NTC's
Super-Mini
BRITISH
SLANG
Dictionary

D1487888

NTC's Super-Mini BRITISH SLANG Dictionary

Ewart James

NTC Publishing Group

Library of Congress Cataloging-in-Publication Data

James, Ewart.
    [Contemporary British slang]
    NTC's super-mini British slang dictionary / Ewart James.
       p.   cm. — (NTC's super-minis)
    Originally published as Contemporary British slang—T.p. verso.
    Includes index.
    ISBN 0-8442-0111-1
    1. English language—Great Britain—Slang—Dictionaries. I. James, Ewart.
II. NTC Publishing Group.   III. Title.   IV. Series.
PE3729.G7S64 2000
427'.941—dc21
                                     99-57958
                                         CIP

Interior design by Terry Stone

Originally published as *Contemporary British Slang*

This edition first published in 2000 by NTC Publishing Group
A division of NTC/Contemporary Publishing Group, Inc.
4255 West Touhy Avenue, Lincolnwood (Chicago), Illinois 60712-1975 U.S.A.
Printed in Canada
International Standard Book Number 0-8442-0111-1
05 06 07 08 09 TRA 20 19 18 17 16 15 14 13 12 11 10 9 8 7 6 5 4 3 2

Contents

About This Dictionary

This dictionary is a resource cataloguing the meanings and usage of frequently used slang expressions in the United Kingdom. It contains expressions that are familiar to many U.K. residents, as well as other expressions that are used primarily within small groups of people. These expressions come from movies, novels, newspaper stories, and everyday conversation.

The entries come from various sources. Many have been collected by college students and other individuals. Standard reference works have been used to verify the meanings and spellings of older material. Most of the examples are concocted and have been edited to exemplify an expression's meaning as concisely as possible. The examples are to be taken as representative of slang usage, not of standard, formal English usage. They are included to illustrate meaning, not to prove the earliest date of print or broadcast dissemination.

Guide to the Use of the Dictionary

Entry heads are alphabetised according to an absolute alphabetical order that ignores all punctuation, spaces, and hyphens. The alphabetising scheme also ignores the articles *a*, *an*, and *the* when these words come at the beginning of the entry.

In some entries, comments direct the user to other entries for additional information through the use of the terms "compare with," "see," and "see also."

Terms and Symbols

□ marks the beginning of an example.

acronym an abbreviation consisting of a set of initials pronounced as a single word, as with *UNESCO*, the United Nations Educational, Scientific, and Cultural Organization.

backslang a slang expression created by reversing a standard English expression or another slang expression. This may be based on either the written (letter-by-letter) or the pronounced version of the expression.

cant the jargon of criminals, originally a secret form of speech employed by denizens of the underworld.

crude normally not suitable in public speech and often considered offensive; best avoided.

disguise an expression that is similar in pronunciation or form, but not in meaning, to the expression for which it stands. A disguise is euphemistic in that its pronunciation or form suggests the expression for which it is a disguise. Rhyming slang and backslang are also types of disguise.

euphemism a euphemistic expression.

euphemistic relatively refined and avoiding the negative connotations of some other expression.

eye-dialect a term which is the phonetic written form of a slang or dialectal pronunciation of a standard English expression.

hobson-jobson a process by which unfamiliar, usually foreign, expressions are replaced with familiar ones which sound similar but are unrelated in meaning. The name "hobson-jobson" originated from a garbled anglicisation of the exclamation "Ya Hasan, ya Husayn!" uttered by Islamic troops of the British Indian Army when on parade during the 19th century. Hasan and Husayn were grandsons of Mohammed.

initialism an abbreviation consisting of the initial letters of the words being shortened. The letters are pronounced one by one, as with *BBC*.

jargon the specialised terminology of an occupation; shoptalk.

offensive occurring in public speech but often considered offensive by individuals so described; use with care.

racially offensive insulting to the group referred to, not acceptable in public speech, and usually considered very offensive; always avoid if possible.

rhyming slang a form of slang where a standard English expression, or its conventional slang equivalent, is replaced by another which rhymes with it but is unconnected in meaning. The replacement may be expanded, the original rhyming portion dropped, and the process repeated from that point. This can result in expressions which lack any apparent connection with their meanings. For example, the rhyming slang term "china" is linked to "friend" as follows: china [plate] ≈ [mate] = friend, where "≈" means that the expressions on either side are linked by rhyme rather than meaning, "=" means that the expressions on either side are linked by meaning rather than rhyme, and a word or phrase contained within [square brackets], as here, is one that is necessary for the link between entry and meaning but is not part of either and is thus silent, although it may not have been at an earlier stage in the evolution of the term to its present-day status. These symbols and this syntax are used throughout the dictionary to show the linkage of rhyming slang expressions.

taboo not acceptable in public speech and usually considered very offensive; always avoid if possible.

term of address an expression that can be used to address someone directly.

underworld from the speech of criminals and often, by osmosis, police officers.

aardvark hard work. (A pun.) □ *What they expect from us here is too much like aardvark.* □ *If you don't like aardvark you won't last long around here.*

Adam and Eve to believe. (Rhyming slang.) □ *I don't think you Adam and Eve me, do you?* □ *Yes, of course I Adam and Eve what you say.*

aereated livid with rage. □ *Calm down! Don't get so aereated!* □ *Helen got really aereated when she heard that Mary won the essay prize.*

afters the last course of a meal. □ *For afters, Mary ordered ice cream.* □ *After we had finished the afters, we were served with coffee.*

afterthought the youngest child of a large family, especially if much younger than all the rest. □ *I suppose you could say that Petra is an afterthought, as she's ten years younger than her sister.* □ *Petra may be an afterthought, but she's our favourite.*

aggro 1. aggravation. □ *Don't give me all that aggro!* □ *Charlie says the police have been giving him aggro again.* **2.** deliberate violence or the threat of it, often by groups of youths. □ *Some youths have been causing a lot of aggro in the neighbourhood.* □ *Charlie says the police threatened him with aggro.* **3.** a problem or difficulty. □ *I've had a lot of aggro trying to make that TV work.* □ *Jane is having aggro with her tax return.*

airs and graces 1. a man's braces. (U.S. suspenders. Rhyming slang.) □ *Bert stood at the top of the stairs in his airs and graces, the very picture of sartorial elegance.* □ *What have you done with me airs and graces, woman?* **2.** artificial or pretentious behaviour. □ *No more of your airs and graces, just get on with it!* □ *Why do you always put on these airs and graces?*

Alf's peed again. Be seeing you. (From the German *auf Wiedersehen*, by hobson-jobson.) □ *Right, I'm on my way. Alf's peed again!* □ *"Alf's peed again," she cried out, and left.*

all gas and gaiters pompous verbosity. □ *Oh, you can ignore him. He's all gas and gaiters.* □ *It's all gas and gaiters here today.*

all-up finished; ruined. □ *That's it all-up. We can go home now.* □ *The business went all-up last year.*

almond (rocks) AND **army rocks** socks. (Rhyming slang.) □ *You should've seen the multicoloured almonds he was wearing.* □ *So I pulled on me army rocks and went off to work.*

anarf fifty pence. (Half of one pound sterling.) □ *That'll be two anarf quid, squire.* □ *Anarf? For what?*

the anchors brakes on a vehicle. □ *He slammed on the anchors and we slid to a halt.* □ *I think this car needs new anchors.*

angels on horseback oysters wrapped in bacon slices. □ *Mmmm! I just love angels on horseback.* □ *We're having some angels on horseback this evening.*

Any joy? Have you succeeded?; Have you had any luck? (Compare with no joy.) □ *I hear you've been seeking a new job. Any joy yet?* □ *Any joy with the lottery?*

apple core twenty pounds sterling. (Rhyming slang, linked as follows: apple core ≈ [score] = twenty pounds.) □ *That'll cost you an apple core, mate.* □ *I'm not handing over apple core for that thing!*

apple fritter bitter beer. (Rhyming slang. This is the most common draught beer sold in English pubs, usually served at room temperature.) □ *A pint of your apple fritter, bartender!* □ *Fancy an apple fritter, mate?*

apples and pears stairs. (Rhyming slang.) □ *She stood at the top of the apples and pears, shouting at him.* □ *Right, you two! Up the apples and pears and straight to bed!*

apples and rice nice. (Rhyming slang. Used ironically.) □ *Oh that's apples and rice, I must say!* □ *Very apples and rice, I don't think. Get lost!*

April showers flowers. (Rhyming slang.) □ *Harry brought me a bunch of April showers!* □ *He's got that stall selling April showers outside the tube station, right?*

army and navy gravy. (Rhyming slang.) □ *Bert likes his army and navy.* □ *Why do they always drown my food in army and navy?*

army rocks See almond (rocks).

arse 1. the anus; the buttocks. (Taboo. A highly offensive word to most people. There are many additional meanings and constructions using this word. It is in fact Standard English, but virtually all applications of it are not.) □ *Get off your arse and on with your work!* □ *Still, it was funny when she slipped in the mud and landed on her arse.* **2.** a despicable or objectionable person. (Taboo.) □ *Get out of here, you arse!* □ *What an arse that woman is.*

Artful Dodger a lodger. (Rhyming slang. The Artful Dodger was a character in Dickens's novel *Oliver Twist*.) □ *So what's the missus up to with the Artful Dodger?* □ *If that Artful Dodger shows his face here again he won't have any face for long, I promise!*

(as) daft as a brush completely crazy. □ *Tom is as daft as a brush, but fun.* □ *They're all daft as a brush in there.*

(as) dry as a basket very thirsty. □ *Got a pint? I'm dry as a basket.* □ *Being as dry as a basket, I took a long cool drink of water.*

(as) easy as taking pennies from a blind man See (as) easy as taking toffee from a child.

(as) easy as taking toffee from a child AND **(as) easy as taking pennies from a blind man** very easy indeed. □ *Stealing the car was as easy as taking toffee from a child.* □ *Well, it may look as easy as taking pennies from a blind man, but I fear there are complications.*

(as) likely as an electric walking stick See (as) likely as a three pound note.

(as) likely as a nine bob note See (as) likely as a three pound note.

(as) likely as a three pound note AND **(as) likely as a nine bob note; (as) likely as an electric walking stick** not very likely; obviously worthless; absurd; bogus. □ *His explanation was as likely as an electric walking stick.* □ *That story is about as likely as a three pound note.*

(as) near as dammit very close indeed; very nearly; almost. (Crude.) □ *Come on! We're as near as dammit, just another inch* *or so!* □ *We're not going to give up when we're as near as dammit to agreement, are we?*

(as) nice as ninepence very tidy; attractive. □ *Yes, very good. It's as nice as ninepence.* □ *I want everything in here nice as ninepence before we leave, ladies.*

(as) safe as houses as safe as can be. □ *Don't worry, you'll be safe as houses here.* □ *Well, I don't feel as safe as houses.*

(as) sharp as a tennis ball AND **(as) sharp as the corners of a round table** exceptionally dumb; very slow-witted. (Ironic.) □ *Yes, I'm afraid Tony is about as sharp as a tennis ball.* □ *The guy's as sharp as the corners of a round table, but very friendly.*

(as) sharp as the corners of a round table See (as) sharp as a tennis ball.

at a good bat at a high speed. □ *The car was moving at a good bat.* □ *"Yes," said the policeman, "it was going at a good bat. Too good."*

at the crease AND **at the wicket** batting. (Cricket.) □ *It's my turn at the crease.* □ *I love my time at the wicket.*

at the wicket See at the crease.

Aunt(y) Beeb AND the **Beeb** the BBC. □ *Aunty Beeb won't ever show that.* □ *The Beeb showed it last night.*

B

baby's head steak and kidney pudding. (From its appearance.) □ *Fancy some baby's head?* □ *Baby's head is always my favourite dish!*

baby's pram jam. (Rhyming slang.) □ *Pass me the baby's pram, please mum.* □ *Jane makes her own baby's pram, you know.*

backhander a clandestine, improper, or secret payment such as a bribe or informal gratuity. □ *Imagine! She offered me a backhander to give her company the contract!* □ *So, just how big a backhander did you get from her?*

backward about coming forward shy. □ *Is he not rather backward about coming forward?* □ *Backward about coming forward? No, not Otto!*

bad fist a bad job. □ *I don't want to make a bad fist of this.* □ *You'll not make a bad fist!*

bad form improper or impolite behaviour. □ *Placing your feet on the boss's desk would definitely be considered bad form.* □ *Bad form is a bad idea around here.*

bad patch a difficult period. □ *I was sorry to hear of your bad patch.* □ *Are you over your bad patch yet?*

bad show **1.** a misfortune. □ *Oh, what a bad show.* □ *Bad show! Better luck next time!* **2.** something done or presented badly. □ *That was a bad show. We must do better next time.* □ *Another bad show like that and there won't be another time.*

bags a large quantity. □ *There's plenty! Bags!* □ *We need bags of the stuff.*

baked bean the Queen; any queen. (Rhyming slang.) □ *Sally likes to watch the baked bean on the telly.* □ *Which particular baked bean are you talking about?*

ball and bat AND **this and that** a hat. (Rhyming slang.) □ *Why are you wearing that ridiculous ball and bat?* □ *I'm going to buy myself a new this and that.*

ballocks AND **bollocks 1.** the testicles. (Taboo.) □ *He turned sideways to protect his bollocks.* □ *Thud, right in the bollocks. Ye gods, it hurt!* **2.** Nonsense!; This is untrue! (Taboo.) □ *That is just ballocks!* □ *Bollocks! You're quite wrong about that.*

ball of chalk See penn'orth (of chalk).

balloon car a saloon bar. (Rhyming slang.) □ *The balloon car's the more expensive area of a traditional pub.* □ *Originally, women were allowed into the balloon car only.*

ballsed up confused; mixed up. (This is hyphenated before a nominal.) □ *That bitch is so ballsed up she doesn't know anything.* □ *This is really a ballsed-up mess you've made.*

bally bloody. (Crude. A euphemism for or variation on bloody.) □ *Get your bally car out of my way!* □ *That was bally stupid!*

band in the box venereal disease. (Rhyming slang, linked as follows: band in the box ≈ [pox] = venereal disease.) □ *All right, it's true, I've got the band in the box.* □ *Getting the band in the box tends to restrict your love life, you know.*

banger a sausage. □ *Have you got any bangers?* □ *Mike always likes a banger or two at breakfast.*

bangers and mash a dish of sausages and mashed potatoes. □ *A serving of bangers and mash over here, please!* □ *Bangers and mash are always acceptable.*

bang off immediately; without delay; right now. □ *I'll be there bang off.* □ *Hurry! I need this bang off.*

bang on 1. to harangue, nag, or remonstrate with someone in an especially lengthy manner. □ *Why are you always banging on?* □ *Because banging on is the only way to get you to do anything.* **2.** AND **smack on** exactly correct; right on the target. □ *Bang on! That's it, exactly.* □ *I'll try to get it smack on the next time, too.*

bang someone up to lock someone away, especially in jail. □ *Otto's been banged up for two years.* □ *They banged Otto up for about twenty years.*

banjaxed 1. demolished; ruined. (Irish usage.) □ *My car is totally banjaxed. What a mess!* □ *Everything I worked for is now banjaxed.* **2.** utterly defeated; totally unable to continue. (Irish usage.) □ *Well, I can do no more. I'm banjaxed.* □ *The rest of us are all banjaxed too.* **3.** amazed; startled; disbelieving. (Irish usage.) □ *No! I'm banjaxed! That's amazing!* □ *We were all banjaxed by the news.* **4.** intoxicated due to drink or drugs. (Irish usage.) □ *Joe and Arthur kept on knocking them back till they were both banjaxed.* □ *She's sort of banjaxed right now.*

banjoed completely intoxicated due to drink or drugs. □ *She just sat there and got banjoed.* □ *All four of them went out and got themselves comprehensively banjoed.*

banker 1. a route regularly requested by taxi-drivers' clients. □ *A couple more bankers and I'm finished for the day.* □ *Heathrow to the City is a typical banker.* **2.** a business transaction that is reliably profitable. □ *Every one of these sales is a banker.* □ *Bankers may be boring, but they'll make you rich.*

barking (mad) completely crazy. □ *You're barking mad!* □ *I think I am going barking.*

Barnaby Rudge a judge. (Rhyming slang. Barnaby Rudge was a character in Dickens's novel of the same name.) □ *I'll be up before the Barnaby Rudge tomorrow.* □ *That Barnaby Rudge ain't wearing no wig!*

barnet hair. (Rhyming slang, linked as follows: Barnet [Fair] ≈ hair. Barnet is a district in north London.) □ *Me barnet's a right mess.* □ *There's nuffink wrong with yer barnet, luv.*

bar steward an odious individual. (Crude. A deliberate alteration and disguise of *bastard*.) □ *You really can be a bar steward at times, Rodney!* □ *I don't care if that bar steward is the Pope in person. Get him out of here!*

basher someone regularly engaged in carrying out uninteresting or boring duties. □ *It must be very boring being a basher.* □ *Well, a lot of bashers don't seem to worry about that.*

bat 1. a step, pace, or speed. □ *You'll get the best results if you can maintain a regular, steady bat.* □ *Try to increase your bat a little. We would rather like to get there this year, you know.* **2.** a price. □ *I'm not paying a bat like that for this.* □ *Come on then, what bat do you really want for it?*

bat and wicket a ticket. (Rhyming slang.) □ *Well, I've got me bat and wicket and I'm going on holiday tomorrow!* □ *You need a bat and wicket to get on the train, love.*

battle cruiser a public house or pub. (Rhyming slang, linked as follows: battle cruiser ≈ [boozer] = pub(lic house).) □ *He's down the battle cruiser, as usual.* □ *That's not a bad little battle cruiser you've got there, mate.*

be a bit slow upstairs See be a bit thick.

be a bit thick 1. to be unacceptable or unreasonable. □ *Hey! That's a bit thick! You can't do that!* □ *I thought the explanation was a bit thick, but what could I do?* **2.** AND **be a bit slow upstairs** to be dim-witted or stupid. □ *Harry's a bit slow upstairs, you know.* □ *All of us can seem to be a bit thick at times.*

beak 1. a nose. □ *What a beak on that guy!* □ *I want some glasses that sit in just the right place on my wonderful beak.* **2.** a judge or magistrate. □ *I'll be up before the beak tomorrow.* □ *The beak ain't wearing a wig!* **3.** a school headmaster. □ *The beak asked the teacher what she thought she was doing.* □ *If you do that again, I'll send you to see the beak!*

beaver away at something to work consistently and well. □ *Oh, they're beavering away at that right now.* □ *Keep beavering away at it until we solve it.*

the **Beeb** See Aunt(y) Beeb.

beer from the wood draught beer drawn from a wooden cask. □ *I prefer beer from the wood.* □ *Beer from the wood has a special flavour.*

beer token See drinking token.

beer voucher See drinking token.

bees (and honey) money. (Rhyming slang.) □ *Sorry, I can't afford it, I've no bees and honey.* □ *How much bees do you need, squire?*

beetle about to scurry around. □ *She's always beetling about.* □ *Why do you have to beetle about all the time?*

beetle-crusher a large shoe or boot. □ *She pulled on her beetle-crushers and left the room, despondent.* □ *These beetle-crushers really do nothing for your appearance, Cynthia.*

be for it to be in immediate danger of punishment or other trouble. □ *You're for it when they catch you!* □ *I'll be for it if I get caught.*

beggar my neighbour unemployed. (Rhyming slang, linked as follows: beggar my neighbour ≈ [labour] = [(no) work] = unemployed.) □ *Harry's beggar my neighbour again.* □ *That beggar my neighbour guy next door was looking for you.*

be light (of) something lacking something; short of something. □ *Yes, he's light of something all right: brains, I think.* □ *The balance sheet's light about £100,000.*

bell a telephone call. □ *I'll give you a bell.* □ *She's been waiting all day for that bell.*

belt and braces especially strong security or safety. □ *Right, let's take no chances. We'll have some real belt and braces here!* □ *Don't you think that's a bit too much like belt and braces, sir?*

belt up to be quiet; to shut up. □ *I'm trying to sleep! Please belt up.* □ *Will you please just belt up.*

beyond it 1. exhausted; unable to continue. □ *I'm sorry, my father's beyond it.* □ *It's been a long day and I'm beyond it.* **2.** incapacitated by drink. □ *Brian was beyond it before closing time.* □ *If you get beyond it you'll be kicked out of the pub.*

BF See bloody fool.

big ben 1. ten pounds sterling. (Rhyming slang. Big Ben is the bell of the clock in the tower of the House of Commons in London.) □ *All right, here's a big ben. Don't spend it all in one shop.* □ *Can you lend me a big ben till pay-day?* **2.** the numeral 10; ten of anything. (Rhyming slang.) □ *I'll give you a quid for big ben of them.* □ *Big ben? You've got that many?*

the **Big Smoke** AND the **Great Smoke; the Smoke** London. □ *I'm off up to the Big Smoke for a business meeting.* □ *I don't like going to the Smoke, but when I must, I must.*

bike it to cycle. □ *He's biking it back home just now.* □ *Bike it over there and tell him we need to talk.*

Billingsgate pheasant AND **Yarmouth capon** a red herring; misleading information; a false clue. □ *I'm afraid that that has turned out to be no more than a Billingsgate pheasant.* □ *We can't afford any more Yarmouth capons. Let's get it right!*

Bill shop a police station. □ *He's gone to the Bill shop to complain.* □ *They've so much business here they're building a new Bill shop.*

bimbo 1. the posterior or bottom. (Dated.) □ *He slipped on the ice and landed on his bimbo.* □ *Sit yourself down on your bimbo and pay attention.* **2.** a glamorous, but silly or empty-headed, young woman. □ *All right, she's a bimbo, but she still has rights. Have a heart!* □ *Now that bimbo is a star in the movies.*

the **bin** a cell in a police station or prison. □ *Bert's in the bin again.* □ *Who's in the bin there, Sarge?*

binder a bore or tiresome person. □ *What's a binder like that doing around here?* □ *I'm sorry but we really don't need another binder working here.*

bind someone to bore or tire someone. □ *My goodness, that fellow binds me!* □ *I think Walter has bound Dad into sleep again!*

bin something to throw away something. □ *Oh, I binned that ages ago.* □ *If it's no use to you, just bin it.*

bish a mistake or error. □ *No more bishes, please!* □ *What a foolish bish that turned out to be!*

a **bit of all right 1.** a satisfactory condition or situation. □ *Yeh, this set-up's a bit of all right, innit?* □ *Now if I was set up in a bit of all right like that, I'd just be quiet.* **2.** an unexpected pleasant event; good luck. □ *Well that was a bit of all right. We should be all right now.* □ *Just one little bit of all right would be nice!*

bits and bobs bits and pieces. □ *We ended up with nothing but bits and bobs to work on.* □ *I have some more bits and bobs here.*

black and tan stout or porter beer mixed with ale in equal proportions. □ *Give my friend here a black and tan.* □ *How about a black and tan before you go, Charlie?*

black and white night. (Rhyming slang.) □ *What were you up to during the black and white?* □ *I was being ill all black and white, that's what I was up to.*

black-coated workers prunes. (A pun on "work," in the sense that prunes, which are dark-coloured, cause the human digestive system to "work." In other words, constipation is avoided or overcome.) □ *He likes his black-coated workers. Keeps things moving along, he says.* □ *Oh no, no black-coated workers for me!*

blackleg a scab or strike-breaker; a betrayer of fellow workers, etc. □ *We're refusing to work with that blackleg.* □ *They brought in blacklegs to break the strike.*

blackwash to make something look worse than it really is; to emphasise something bad. □ *Look, things are hard enough without the likes of you blackwashing them.* □ *Well, it looks as if the blackwashing has started.*

bladder of lard a playing card. (Rhyming slang.) □ *Come on, what's that bladder of lard we can see in your hand?* □ *Have you got any other bladders of lard hidden away?*

blagger 1. a violent thief or mugger. □ *I was stopped by a blagger.* □ *The police caught the blagger.* **2.** a scrounger. □ *The blaggers who hang around outside the railway station were rounded up by the police today.* □ *Since John lost his job, he's turned into nothing more than a blagger.*

blag someone to mug someone; to rob someone in a violent way. □ *A gang of youths were prowling around blagging people.* □ *He blagged an old lady and got put away for six months.*

blag something to steal or to scrounge something. □ *He blagged some food from the little man again, you know!* □ *Why do you keep blagging money off me?*

blank someone to ignore someone. □ *Why are you blanking me?* □ *The hostess and all the guests blanked him, until he began to wonder if he was invisible or something.*

blasted damned. □ *I asked her to get her blasted stockings off the shower curtain.* □ *Shut your blasted mouth!*

bleat (to make) a feeble protest. □ *Oh stop bleating, will you!* □ *There's Harry, making his usual bleats.*

bleeder an unattractive or disreputable person. (Crude.) □ *This bleeder is offensive most of the time.* □ *Who's the bleeder with the enormous moustache?*

bleeding AND **blessed** bloody. (A euphemism or variation. Crude.) □ *Get that bleeding dog out of my nice house!* □ *Oh my, what a blessed mess!*

blessed See bleeding.

blighter an insignificant man. □ *What does the blighter want?* □ *He's a rather surprising blighter.*

Blighty England. (From the Hindi *bilayati*, meaning "foreign," by hobson-jobson.) □ *After all these years in far-flung corners of the globe dreaming of Blighty, all he wanted was to come home.* □ *When he eventually got back to Blighty, I think the reality was a bit of a shock.*

blimey AND **corblimey; gorblimey** a euphemistic abbreviation and disguise of *God blind me*, once a popular oath. (Crude.) □ *Blimey, that's a nice car.* □ *Well, gorblimey, I'm not interested in that!*

blind (along) to drive heedlessly and very rapidly, especially without looking ahead. □ *If you blind along like that you'll have a serious accident.* □ *Don't blind like that, please. It makes me very nervous.*

blinder an extensive drinking session. □ *I think the boys are off on another blinder.* □ *I'm getting to be too old for these blinders.*

blinding AND **blinking; blooming** bleeding; bloody. (A euphemism and disguise. Crude.) □ *Why don't you take your blinding job and shove it?* □ *That's a blooming stupid idea.*

blind someone with science to confuse or impress someone with a lengthy or complex explanation, especially a technical or scientific-sounding one. □ *I'm blinded with science. What's really going on here?* □ *Well, now you've got me really blinded with science.*

blinking See **blinding**.

blistering bloody. (Crude. A euphemism.) □ *That car is blistering fast.* □ *Who's the blistering fool who did this?*

blob 1. an ulcer. □ *I think you've got a little blob here, Mr Simpson.* □ *That's an ugly blob. I want rid of it.* **2.** the victim of a fatal highway accident. (Police slang.) □ *There were two blobs lying in the road.* □ *How many blobs were there this time?* **3.** a score of zero runs scored by a cricket batsman. □ *Another blob again I see, Gerald. Sorry.* □ *I really must try to do better than a blob next time.*

blobwagon an ambulance attending a road traffic accident. (Police and medical.) □ *Send for a blobwagon!* □ *When the blobwagon got there, it was too late.*

bloke a man. (As distinct from a woman. Reputedly derived from a secret word used by gypsies.) □ *Ask that bloke if he needs any help.* □ *Why do we need this bloke?*

blokey rumbustiously masculine. □ *Oh, he's very friendly in a blokey sort of way.* □ *I feel sort of out of place among all that blokey heartfulness.*

bloody very. (An intensifier. Crude.) □ *Well, that's bloody unlikely, I'd say.* □ *He can be bloody annoying at times, I agree.*

bloody fool AND **BF** a very foolish person. (Crude.) □ *I felt like such a bloody fool when I found out that I'd got onto the wrong train.* □ *Tell that BF in the front row to shut up.*

bloody-minded deliberately awkward, perverse, or unhelpful. □ *Why do you always have to be so bloody-minded?* □ *He may be bloody-minded, but I'm afraid he's right.*

bloomer a mistake. □ *Rubbing my nose in it is not going to correct the bloomer.* □ *So I made a bloomer! I wish you'd stop going on about it!*

blooming See blinding.

blot one's copybook to make a mistake; to create a bad impression or damage one's reputation. □ *How could I ever have blotted my copybook like that?* □ *I don't intend to blot my copybook.*

blower a telephone. □ *The blower's been very busy all day today.* □ *The blower was ringing off the hook when I came in.*

blow the gaff to expose or tell a secret by accident. □ *Why did you have to blow the gaff?* □ *Blowing the gaff at this very moment is particularly awkward.*

blue 1. pertaining or relating to the Conservative Party (in the U.K.). □ *He's another blue individual, if ever I saw one.* □ *The blue vote is slipping away this time round.* **2.** depressed; melancholy. □ *I'm feeling sort of blue.* □ *That music always makes me blue.* □ *I'm in a blue mood.* **3.** a police officer; the police. □ *The blues will be here in a minute.* □ *One blue isn't enough to handle this job.* **4.** a wild party. □ *Sam invited us to a blue, but we're getting a little old for that kind of thing.* □ *After a blue, I couldn't keep my eyes open the following day.*

bluebottle a policeman. (From the colour of his uniform.) □ *See that bluebottle over there? He lifted me once.* □ *The bluebottles will catch up with you some day.*

blue moon a spoon. (Rhyming slang.) □ *Hoy, waiter! Where's me blue moon then?* □ *You're supposed to lick the blue moon clean Nigel, not yer actual bowl.*

blue murder loud cries of alarm; a great noise. □ *What a noise! The child was crying blue murder.* □ *There was someone yelling blue murder all day long.*

blue o'clock the wee small hours; the dead of night. □ *Why are you up at blue o'clock?* □ *She came home at blue o'clock. I wonder why?*

blunderbuss a baby's pram. (A pun.) □ *If you're having a baby, you'll need a blunderbuss.* □ *Well, my aunt bought me a blunderbuss for the new baby.*

board of green cloth 1. a billiards table. □ *The balls were set up for play on the board of green cloth again.* □ *Here was the board of green cloth, ready for another game of billiards.* **2.** a card table. □ *The four sat silently around the board of green cloth. No one spoke.* □ *A game of whist? Right, let's get out the board of green cloth.*

boat race a face. (Rhyming slang.) □ *Why are you looking at me like that? Is there something wrong with me boat race?* □ *The woman had a very unusual boat race, you know.*

bob (and dick) unwell. (Rhyming slang, linked as follows: Bob (and Dick) ≈ [sick] = unwell.) □ *God, I feel really bob and dick!* □ *I told you that curry would make you bob.*

bobby a policeman. (From the given name of Sir Robert Peel, who founded the Metropolitan Police in 1829.) □ *The bobby broke up the fight.* □ *These two bobbies drove around in their car picking on innocent people like me.*

bobby-dazzler an excellent or unusual person or thing. □ *This is a bobby-dazzler of a day!* □ *Mary's got herself a bobby-dazzler of a new job.*

bod 1. someone who is intrusive, supercilious, or tedious. (An abbreviation of *body*.) □ *So this bod, a total stranger, turns round and tells Mary that he thinks her skirt doesn't suit her!* □ *Frank's a funny old bod, always pontificating on the topic of the day—whatever it happens to be.* **2.** a person. (An abbreviation of *body*.) □ *How many bods are coming over tonight?* □ *Who's the bod with the tight slacks?*

bodge to botch or bungle. □ *I really bodged this before.* □ *I hope I don't bodge it up this time.*

bodgy not functioning properly; inferior. □ *That sort of behaviour is really too bodgy to be acceptable, you know.* □ *Sorry, it's too bodgy for me.*

bodice ripper a romantic novel containing much titillation, which is aimed at female readers. □ *Margo just devours bodice rippers, reading one after the other.* □ *I can't get into reading bodice rippers. Sorry.*

body-snatcher a stretcher-bearer. □ *He's got a job as a body-snatcher at the local hospital.* □ *The body-snatchers carried her off to the ambulance.*

boff the buttocks. □ *There is some mustard or something on your boff.* □ *She fell right on her boff.*

bog a toilet. (Crude.) □ *I must use your bog!* □ *Help yourself. The bog's through there.*

bog-ignorant very ignorant or stupid. (Offensive. From the supposed stupidity of the supposedly bog-dwelling Irish.) □ *I think that was the most bog-ignorant suggestion yet heard. Next?* □ *Get out, you bog-ignorant Irish git!*

bog off to leave; to go away. □ *Look, why don't you just bog off?* □ *You know, I finally told him to bog off and he did!*

bog-roll a roll of toilet paper. (Crude.) □ *We need a bog-roll in here!* □ *There should be a bog-roll in the cupboard.*

bog-standard standard; normal; unmodified. □ *Yes, that's the bog-standard model you have there.* □ *I'm just looking for a bog-standard one—nothing fancy.*

bog up to make a mess of things. □ *I think I've bogged up again.* □ *Why do you always bog up anything that matters?*

bogy a policeman. □ *Think about how the bogy on the beat is affected by this cold.* □ *The bogy stopped at the door, tried the lock, and moved on.*

boiler an unattractive or stupid woman, especially an older one. □ *I'm afraid she really is an old boiler.* □ *The boiler seemed to be unable to understand what was happening.*

bollocking AND **rollocking** a severe chastisement. □ *I think you can be sure that if you don't behave you will experience a right* *bollocking.* □ *We could hear the rollocking at the other end of the building.*

bollocks See ballocks.

B.O.L.T.O.P. AND **BOLTOP** Better on lips than on paper. (The initialism is sometimes written on love letters, set beside a "paper kiss"—that is, an X. Also an acronym.) □ *XXXX B.O.L.T.O.P.* □ *Love and kisses. BOLTOP.*

bonce 1. a large glass marble used for playing various games. □ *The children like to use a bonce when they play marbles.* □ *Bonces made of multicoloured glass can be very pretty.* **2.** the head. □ *Put your hat on your bonce, and let's go.* □ *That's using your bonce!*

bone box the mouth. □ *Have I ever told you that you have an ugly bone box?* □ *Shut your bone box and get on with your work.*

bone dome a protective helmet worn by motorcyclists, aviators, etc. □ *It's an offence to ride on a motor bike without wearing a bone dome.* □ *He grabbed his bone dome and climbed into the cockpit of the Tornado.*

boob tube a woman's tight strapless dress top. □ *I don't think she suits that boob tube.* □ *She came out to see me wearing a boob tube.*

booby-prize AND **wooden spoon** a prize, usually mythical, awarded to the last in a race, competition, etc. □ *I see Simon's won the booby-prize again this year.* □ *Well, I would not like to say that you've come last, but here's your wooden spoon.*

booed and hissed intoxicated due to drink. (Crude. Rhyming slang, linked as follows: booed and hissed ≈ [pissed] = drunk. Compare with **Brahms and Liszt** and **Mozart**.) □ *Joe and Arthur kept on knocking them back till they were both booed and hissed.* □ *Boy, I was really booed and hissed. I'll never drink another drop.*

boot 1. the **boot** a dismissal or ejection. □ *I got the boot even though I had worked there for a decade.* □ *Seven people got the boot there this week.* **2.** money. □ *How much boot do you need, then?* □ *Sorry, I can't afford it, I've no boot.* **3.** a car tyre. (Usually in the plural.) □ *I'm looking for a new set of boots for my car.* □ *You'll get a good price for boots here.* **4.** to start the operating system of a computer. (Computer jargon.) □ *I tried to boot the thing, but it just sat there.* □ *It booted all right, but when I tried to run the application it just beeped at me.*

booter a merchant or trader at a car boot sale. □ *This booter was selling used false teeth, would you believe!* □ *Harry's working weekends as a booter.*

the **boot is on the other foot** things have changed around. □ *Well, the boot is on the other foot, so watch out!* □ *Now that the new management has taken over, the boot is on the other foot.*

boot sale See car boot sale.

bootsy a hotel porter. □ *The bootsy here will be happy to carry your luggage to your room, madam.* □ *The bootsy put the luggage down in the room and stood silently with his hand out, waiting.*

booze 1. to drink alcohol to excess; to go on a bash. □ *Let's go out boozing.* □ *Stop boozing for a minute and listen to me, guys.* **2.** an alcohol beverage. (Slang since the 1500s.) □ *I don't care for booze. It makes me sneeze.* □ *Where's the booze?*

bo-peep sleep. (Rhyming slang.) □ *I could use about another hour of bo-peep.* □ *It's about time to get some bo-peep.*

borassick broke; entirely without money. □ *Me? Lend you money? I'm borassick!* □ *I was borassick by the end of the week, but it was well worth it.*

borrow and beg an egg. (Rhyming slang.) □ *A sausage and borrow and beg please, mate.* □ *I'm telling you, he balanced a borrow and beg on the end of his nose!*

boss shot 1. a bad guess. □ *Yes it was a boss shot, but then I really had no idea.* □ *I hope this is not another of your boss shots.* **2.** a failed attempt. □ *Oh no, another boss shot!* □ *That last boss shot was particularly disastrous.* **3.** a mess. □ *What a boss shot you've made of this!* □ *We don't need any more boss shots, you know.*

bossy-boots a domineering or bossy woman or child. □ *Please get that bossy-boots out of here!* □ *This particular bossy-boots has just been sacked, as it happens.*

bottle courage or self-confidence. □ *Oh, he's got lots of bottle all right.* □ *It must take a lot of bottle to do that.*

bottle and stopper a policeman. (Rhyming slang, linked as follows: bottle and stopper ≈ [copper] = policeman.) □ *The bottle and stopper stopped at the door, tried the lock, and moved on.* □ *Think about how the bottle and stopper on the beat is affected by this cold.*

bottle of beer an ear. (Rhyming slang.) □ *Look at the huge bottle of beers on her!* □ *Allow me to take you to one side and have a word in your bottle of beer, sonny.*

bottle of sauce a horse. (Rhyming slang.) □ *He said I should take a both-way bet on that bottle of sauce.* □ *Who ever told you that that bottle of sauce had any hope of winning?*

bottle of Scotch a watch. (Rhyming slang.) □ *That's a new bottle of Scotch on your wrist, innit?* □ *Where did you get your bottle of Scotch, then?*

bottle of water a daughter. (Rhyming slang.) □ *Careful there, mate! That's old Bert's bottle of water!* □ *Me bottle of water's coming round later today.*

bottle out to lose one's nerve. □ *I'm afraid he's going to bottle out rather than take the risk.* □ *Don't you dare bottle out on me again!*

bottom 1. the buttocks. □ *Ted fell on his bottom and just sat there.* □ *My bottom is sore from sitting too long.* **2.** to clean especially thoroughly. □ *You had better bottom this properly if you want to get paid.* □ *I have bottomed the thing twice now, and still she wants it cleaner!*

bottom of the garden the point in a rear garden that is farthest from the house. □ *There was a shed at the bottom of the garden.* □ *They wandered off down to the bottom of the garden, I think.*

bouncer a cheque which is returned unpaid. □ *His cheque turned out to be a bouncer, I'm afraid.* □ *That's about the twentieth bouncer he's issued recently.*

bovver bother; trouble. (Eye-dialect. Typical spoken English in London and surrounding area. Used in writing only for effect. Used in the examples of this dictionary.) □ *There's been some bovver down at the pub, I hear.* □ *Bert's in a spot of bovver with the rozzers again.*

bovver boot a heavy boot, often with a metal toe cap, worn by **bovver boys**. □ *Traditionally, it's yer bovver boy what wears yer bovver boots.* □ *Why do you wear bovver boots?*

bovver boy a violent troublemaker. □ *There was a group of bovver boys standing around outside the pub.* □ *Little Archie's turned into a regular bovver boy, I'm afraid.*

bow and arrow 1. a sparrow. (Rhyming slang.) □ *Aw, look at the little bow and arrow over there.* □ *Someone just shot the pretty bow and arrow with a bow and arrow!* **2.** a barrow. (Rhyming slang.) □ *A man passed by, pushing a bow and arrow.* □ *The bow and arrow was loaded down with fresh fruit.*

box See idiot box.

box clever to behave shrewdly. □ *I tried to box clever, but she was too smart for me.* □ *Box clever with this one. He's out to trip you up.*

boy in blue stew. (Rhyming slang.) □ *Any more of that great boy in blue, love?* □ *Harry always likes me boy in blue.*

boys on ice lice. (Rhyming slang.) □ *The first thing is to check for boys on ice on everyone.* □ *I'm afraid all of these refugees have boys on ice.*

Brahms and Liszt intoxicated due to drink. (Rhyming slang, linked as follows: Brahms and Liszt ≈ [pissed] = drunk. Compare with booed and hissed and Mozart.) □ *Tracy gets a little Brahms and Liszt after a drink or two.* □ *Tipsy? Brahms and Liszt, more like!*

brainbox a very intelligent person. □ *Here was one brainbox that was different from the others, he thought.* □ *I don't think I could take another brainbox like that today.*

brass 1. cheekiness. □ *Why, the brass of her!* □ *Less of your brass, you young pup!* **2.** money. □ *I don't make enough brass to go on a trip like that!* □ *It takes a lot of brass to buy a car like that.* **3.** a badge, medallion, or ornament. □ *Right, you go round the building and polish all the brass you can find.* □ *Remember to wear your brass at the parade tomorrow.*

brass band a hand. (Rhyming slang.) □ *He had a brass band on him like a gorilla.* □ *Get your brass bands off me glass.*

brass farthing the least possible money. □ *Look, I don't have so much as two brass farthings to rub together.* □ *I'm afraid there is not even one brass farthing left in that account.*

brass monkey's weather very cold weather. (Crude. Derived from the picturesque description of such weather as being ". . . so cold it would freeze the balls off a brass monkey.") □ *Cor! Real brass monkey's weather today, innit?* □ *In brass monkey's weather like this he prefers to stay indoors.*

brass neck AND **hard neck; neck** cheek; impudence. □ *The brass neck! Who does she think she is?* □ *Any more neck like that and he'll get everything he deserves.*

brass something out to brazen something out. □ *What else could I do but brass it out?* □ *I tried to brass the situation out but did not have the nerve.*

brass up to pay up. □ *Come on, brass up!* □ *Time to brass up, is it?*

brave and bold cold. (Rhyming slang.) □ *I won't go out in brave and bold weather.* □ *Why does it have to be so brave and bold?*

bread and butter a gutter. (Rhyming slang.) □ *John! The bread and butter's overflowing again!* □ *I've got to get the ladder out to fix the bread and butter.*

bread (and honey) money. (Rhyming slang.) □ *I need to get some bread and honey to live on.* □ *You got any bread you can spare?*

bread and lard hard. (Rhyming slang.) □ *Cor, that's a bread and lard job you've got there!* □ *The ice was really bread and lard.*

breeze an outburst of bad temper. □ *That one remark was enough to cause the whole subsequent breeze.* □ *What a breeze that was! I thought murder might be done!*

brekkies breakfast. (Jocular or childish.) □ *Anyone want brekkies?* □ *Ah, brekkies! What do we have?*

brickie a bricklayer. □ *We need more brickies if we're to get this thing built on time.* □ *There's a brickie here to see you.*

bridge widow a wife left alone while her husband plays bridge. (Compare with golf widow.) □ *Why don't you come along to the next meeting of the Bridge Widows?* □ *There's a lot of us bridge widows around here, especially at weekends.*

brief 1. material pertaining to legal case-work performed by a barrister. □ *I've got an interesting brief for you to consider.* □ *I'm not sure how we stand on that brief.* **2.** a criminal barrister. □ *Get me my brief!* □ *The brief says he'll be here in an hour.*

bright spark a lively, cheerful person. □ *Even a bright spark like that has to earn a living.* □ *What does the bright spark want?*

brill excellent; thrilling. □ *Boy, this fishing rod is brill!* □ *This wine is really brill!*

bring someone low to humiliate or ruin. □ *Now that sort of disaster always brings me low.* □ *Why do you try to bring low your friends?*

bring someone to book to charge someone with a crime, especially when this is done by the police. □ *They are determined to bring Mr Big to book.* □ *The only ones they ever bring to book are the little men.*

bristols the female breasts. (Crude. Rhyming slang, linked as follows: Bristol [Citie]s ≈ [titties] = breasts. Bristol City is a soccer club.) □ *There she was, bold as brass, with her bristols on full display.* □ *My bristols aren't all I might have wished for.*

Brixton briefcase a portable stereo radio, especially a large, powerful one that is played very loudly. (Potentially racially offensive. Brixton, in south London, has a large population of immigrants from the Caribbean and Africa.) □ *Turn off your Brixton briefcase for a moment and just listen to what I have to tell you.* □ *When you get several Brixton briefcases all together, the noise is indescribable.*

broad brush without any detail; general. □ *This is the broad brush picture.* □ *I only have broad brush information—no detail.*

broads playing-cards. □ *Get out the broads and we'll have a game.* □ *What do you like to play with your broads?*

broadsman a card sharper. □ *Broadsmen can make a lot of money out of the dupes they persuade to play with them.* □ *That friendly old card partner you've found is a broadsman, I'm sure.*

brolly an umbrella. □ *I'm taking my brolly as it looks like rain.* □ *He opened his brolly and walked out into the rain.*

brothel creepers thickly soled suede shoes. (Crude.) □ *The trouble with brothel creepers is that they make the wearer so silent.* □ *He put on his brothel creepers and went out into the rain.*

brown bread dead. (Rhyming slang.) □ *Me missus is brown bread, mate.* □ *He put the brown bread cat in the rubbish bin.*

browned off 1. angry. □ *I am really browned off at you!* □ *The boss is browned off—to say the least.* **2.** AND **cheesed off** bored or fed up. □ *I am very browned off today.* □ *Why are you always so cheesed off?*

Brussels sprout a boy scout. (Rhyming slang.) □ *Were you ever a Brussels sprout?* □ *What is that Brussels sprout doing here?*

bubble AND **double bubble** overtime. □ *There's lots of bubble while this rush lasts.* □ *I'm working double bubble tonight again.*

bubble and squeak 1. meat, vegetables, and potatoes chopped up and then fried together. □ *Bubble and squeak is an old favourite in the East End of London.* □ *It's called bubble and squeak because that's what it's supposed to do while it's cooking.* **2.** to speak. (Rhyming slang.) □ *Why did you have to bubble and squeak just then?* □ *Listen to him bubbling and squeaking on and on about nothing!*

bucket and pail a jail. (Rhyming slang.) □ *Get me out of this terrible bucket and pail!* □ *Do you want to talk, or do you want to spend a little time in the bucket and pail?*

Buck House Buckingham Palace. □ *You'll find Buck House at the end of the Mall.* □ *Buck House is the Royal Family's official residence in London.*

bucks See dollars.

buckshee 1. extra or free. (From the Persian *baksis*, meaning "gift," by hobson-jobson.) □ *That particular one is buckshee.* □ *If it's buckshee, there has to be a catch.* **2.** a bribe. □ *He took the buckshee and won't get in our way.* □ *Someone in here has been taking buckshee.*

buck up to cheer up; to perk up. □ *Come on, now, buck up. Things can't be all that bad.* □ *She began to buck up when I showed her the results of the tests.*

buffer See old buffer.

bugger 1. a very serious or difficult problem or predicament. (Taboo.) □ *This is a bugger! What do we do now?* □ *If we don't get this bugger sorted out, the whole project will fail.* **2.** a sodomite. (The official, legal word for a person who engages in sodomy. Nevertheless, the word is normally taboo outside a courtroom.) □ *He is, quite literally, a bugger.* □ *When a judge calls you a bugger, Simon, he is not swearing at you.*

buggin's turn selection by rote rather than merit. □ *We do these things by buggin's turn round here.* □ *It's buggin's turn: you're next!*

bugladders side-whiskers or sideburns. □ *He's the fellow with the great big bugladders.* □ *I don't trust men with bugladders.*

bugs bunny money. (Rhyming slang.) □ *Sorry, I can't afford it. I've no bugs bunny.* □ *How much bugs bunny do you need, then?*

bulge a nose. □ *How did you get a bulge like that?* □ *He threatened to punch me right on the bulge!*

bulge-duster a handkerchief. □ *There was a bulge-duster sticking out of his top pocket.* □ *He removed his bulge-duster and blew his nose.*

bulge the onionbag to score a goal during a game of soccer. □ *Yes, he's bulged the onionbag again! What a goal!* □ *Right lads, let's go out there and bulge the onionbag.*

bull 1. nonsense; bullshit. □ *That's just a lot of bull.* □ *Don't give me that bull! I won't buy it.* **2.** the bull's-eye of a target. □ *Aim at the bull and gently squeeze the trigger.* □ *I hit the bull!*

bull and cow a row; an argument. (Rhyming slang.) □ *No more bull and cows, you two!* □ *I've just had a big bull and cow with Sandra.*

the **Bulldog Breed** the British, as seen by the British. □ *I'm afraid I don't think the Bulldog Breed is quite so bulldog-like any more.* □ *Of course we're the Bulldog Breed, as tough and determined and resilient as ever.*

bullock to pawn something. (Rhyming slang, linked as follows: bullock['s horn] ≈ pawn.) □ *He had no money and had to bullock something.* □ *Why did you ever think to bullock that?*

bull's-eye a hard, large, spherical, peppermint-flavoured sweet or candy. □ *Mummy, can I have a bull's-eye?* □ *I love bull's-eyes. I always have, ever since I was little.*

bum the buttocks. □ *Bob fell down on his bum.* □ *I was so angry. I wanted to kick him in the bum as he left.*

bum bag a small bag attached by a belt around the waist. □ *Why are you wearing a bum bag?* □ *A bum bag is a very handy way to secure your valuables as you travel about.*

bumbledom pompous or officious rules or regulations, or the application of these. (From an officious character called Bumble, in Dickens's novel *Oliver Twist*.) □ *I've just experienced a* *classic case of bumbledom at the local council office.* □ *I think they're sent away to learn how to be better at bumbledom.*

bumf AND **bumph 1.** toilet paper. (Crude.) □ *We need some bumf in here!* □ *There should be some bumph in the cupboard.* **2.** trashy literature. □ *He never reads anything but bumf.* □ *Where do you get that bumph?*

bum-freezer a short coat or jacket. □ *You'll discover why they're called bum-freezers if you wear one on a really cold day.* □ *He stood there in his bum-freezer and shivered.*

bumph See bumf.

bunce 1. a windfall or unexpected profit. □ *Well, here's a nice bit of bunce.* □ *We made a lot of bunce out of that deal.* **2.** commission; profit. □ *No, that's just my regular bunce.* □ *I need that weekly bunce to live on.*

bunce someone to overcharge someone. □ *Those car repair places can bunce you if you don't watch out.* □ *You are trying to bunce me. I won't pay it!*

bunch of fives 1. a handful of five pound notes. □ *He showed me a bunch of fives and said, "Okay, how much if I pay cash?"* □ *He put a bunch of fives into the top pocket of my shirt and said that there were plenty more to be had if I asked no questions.* **2.** the fist. □ *How would you like a bunch of fives right in the kisser?* □ *He ended up with a bunch of fives in the gut.*

bun fight a tea party. □ *The bun fight was most enjoyable.* □ *What a boring bun fight!*

bung 1. to bribe or tip someone. □ *I'm sure you can bung at least one of them, if you try hard enough.* □ *Why do you want one of them bunged?* **2.** to fling or throw something. □ *She was bunging all her old clothes away.* □ *When I said you should get rid of it, I did not mean you should literally bung it out the window.*

bungaloid like a bungalow. □ *It's a single-storey, bungaloid structure.* □ *He hides all day in his bungaloid office.*

bungaloid growth an infestation of bungalows. □ *There has been a bungaloid growth to the west of the town.* □ *We're not going to allow any more bungaloid growth around this area.*

Bungalow Bill a slow-witted man. (Implying that there is nothing much going on upstairs.) □ *What does this dumb Bungalow Bill* *want?* □ *I don't think the Bungalow Bill really knows what he wants.*

bung-full AND **chock-full** full to the top. □ *The boot's bung-full. There's no more room.* □ *The new musical is just chock-full with laughs.*

bung something over to pass or hand something to someone. □ *Bung that manual over, please.* □ *He asked me to bung the thing over.*

bungy a rubber eraser. □ *I've lost my bungy.* □ *Here, take my bungy. I never need it.*

bunk off to play truant, especially from school. □ *Do you have a problem with kids bunking off at this school?* □ *No, no one bunks off here.*

bunny to talk or chatter. (Rhyming slang, linked as follows: bunny = [rabbit (and pork)] ≈ [talk] = chatter.) □ *Why must you bunny like that?* □ *Oh, they're always bunnying about something.*

Bunter any grossly overweight youth. (Offensive. Sometimes used as a term of address. From a fictional schoolboy, Billy Bunter, who appeared in a large number of stories written by Frank Richards between 1910 and the outbreak of World War II.) □ *Fat? He was, let's face it, a real Bunter.* □ *Don't you dare call me Bunter!*

B.U.R.M.A. AND **BURMA** Be upstairs ready my angel. (The initialism is sometimes written on love letters. Also an acronym.) □ *Don't ever forget, B.U.R.M.A.* □ *BURMA, forever.*

Burton(-on-Trent) rent. (Rhyming slang.) □ *That money is for the Burton-on-Trent.* □ *How much is your Burton?*

bushel the throat. (Rhyming slang, linked as follows: bushel [and peck] ≈ [neck] = throat.) □ *I've got a real sore bushel today.* □ *Otto grabbed him by the bushel. He nearly croaked.*

the **business** the best; the genuine one. □ *Now this is the best—the real business.* □ *She always has the business.*

busk it to improvise, especially in a musical context. □ *Let's busk it and see how it goes.* □ *If you're going to be busking it, could you use that room over there?*

butchers a look or glance. (Rhyming slang, linked as follows: butcher's [hook] ≈ look. Usually used with *take a.*) □ *Take a* *butchers at that, John.* □ *He took a butchers at the girl, but didn't recognise her.*

buttons a page boy dressed in livery. □ *Ask the buttons to get me a newspaper.* □ *Imagine. Still with buttons in this day and age!*

butty a sandwich made using a buttered bread roll rather than two slices of bread. (North of England usage.) □ *He sat there, eating a butty.* □ *Can I have a butty, mum?*

by a long chalk by a long way. □ *You've missed by a long chalk.* □ *Not by a long chalk! No way!*

by a short head 1. in a horse race, leading or winning by a very small margin. (Referring to the length of a horse's head.) □ *Silent Runner won the 3.30 at Doncaster by a short head.* □ *The horse won by a short head only, but still, it won!* **2.** very slightly ahead or better than. □ *If Paul is better than Peter, then it's only by a short head.* □ *The difference may only be by a short head, but that's enough here.*

by return by return of post. □ *Please reply by return.* □ *The answer came back by return.*

C

cabbage 1. money. (Originally underworld.) □ *How much cabbage do you want for this heater?* □ *I don't make enough cabbage to go on a trip like that!* **2.** someone who is inactive, disinterested, or apathetic. □ *I'm sorry but I feel like a cabbage just now.* □ *Just ignore the cabbages.* **3.** someone who is brain-dead as the result of illness, accident, etc. (Compare with **cabbage patch**.) □ *I think we have to face facts—he's a cabbage now.* □ *I don't accept that anybody can be reduced to a sort of cabbage.*

cabbage patch a hospital intensive care unit. (See **cabbage**, sense 3.) □ *A lot of nurses work in the cabbage patch.* □ *Visiting the cabbage patch is always so depressing.*

cack-handed 1. left-handed. □ *So I'm cack-handed. So what?* □ *Paul doesn't like people commenting on his being cack-handed.* **2.** clumsy or incompetent. □ *Well, that's a cack-handed way of going about it.* □ *Why are you always so cack-handed?*

caff a café. □ *I'm hungry and here's a caff. Let's use it.* □ *The caff was deserted, and when we ate there we discovered why.*

Camford an alternate combined name to the better-known **Oxbridge** for the Universities of Cambridge and Oxford taken together. (Compare with **Oxbridge**.) □ *I don't know whether he went to Oxford or Cambridge but it was one or the other. Let's just settle for Camford, eh?* □ *There is a sort of Camford mentality which some think is bad for British business.*

cannon to collide. □ *We cannoned into each other on the stairs.* □ *Try to avoid cannoning, all right?*

Cape of Good Hope soap. (Rhyming slang.) □ *What have you done with the Cape of Good Hope, woman?* □ *Some Cape of Good Hope, please. I want to wash.*

Captain Cook AND **cook 1.** a book. (Rhyming slang.) □ *Any good Captain Cooks to read?* □ *Hey, leave me cook alone!* **2.** a look.

(Rhyming slang.) □ *He took a Captain Cook at the girl, but didn't recognise her.* □ *Take a cook at that, Walter.*

car boot sale AND **boot sale** a sale, usually at the weekend or a public holiday, of used or home-made goods, originally from the boot of a car. □ *Fancy visiting the car boot sale this Sunday?* □ *He goes to boot sales in the hope of finding a bargain.*

cardboard box venereal disease. (Rhyming slang, linked as follows: cardboard box ≈ [pox] = venereal disease.) □ *Getting cardboard box does tend to restrict your love life, since you ask.* □ *A dose of the cardboard box is not really funny, you know.*

cards an employee's documents, which are normally held by the employer. □ *I knew I was being sacked because he told me I could just go and collect my cards.* □ *When you come to work here, we will keep your cards in the main office.*

carpet to reprimand. □ *I'm afraid that after that little exhibition, you will have to be carpeted.* □ *I was really carpeted this morning.*

carpet-biter someone who has or tends to have uncontrollable rages. □ *Boy! What a carpet-biter!* □ *Take care, this guy can be a real carpet-biter, you know.*

carry-on 1. a love affair. □ *It seems Jane and Jack are having a carry-on.* □ *Right, there shall be no carry-ons between staff personnel, okay?* **2.** dubious behaviour. □ *What sort of carry-on is going on here?* □ *I think there had been some kind of carry-on just before we arrived.* **3.** a confused or excited environment. □ *What a carry-on that place has become.* □ *I could not work in a carry-on like that.*

carry one's bat to remain in play as a batsman at the end of an innings. (Cricket.) □ *At least, he carried his bat.* □ *It's important for the team that Simon carry his bat tonight.*

carry someone to do someone's work for someone. □ *If you imagine I'm going to carry you, think again.* □ *How did she talk you into carrying her?*

carsey AND **carzey; kahsi; kharsie; khazi 1.** a water closet; a toilet. (Crude. Probably derived from *casa*, meaning "house" in Spanish, which was a slang term for a brothel in 17th- and 18th-century London.) □ *Where's the carsey?* □ *The khazi? Oh, it's along that passageway.* **2.** a communal toilet. (Crude. Typically found in military barracks and similar places.) □ *If you want a* *smoke, go to the carzey.* □ *I went to the kharsie for a quick smoke and met the captain doing the same thing!*

carve something up to ruin someone's chances. □ *You've carved up my chances.* □ *She's saying he's carved up all her plans.*

carve-up 1. a fight; a war. □ *Right men, this is it—the real carve-up.* □ *I'm glad the inevitable carve-up has come at last, really.* **2.** the value of a will. □ *When mother died, all he was interested in was the carve-up.* □ *Always asking about the carve-up is really sick, Otto.* **3.** a swindle. □ *Gerry has a new money-making carve-up, but he hasn't made any yet.* □ *What sort of carve-up did you get ripped off with?*

carving knife a wife. (Rhyming slang.) □ *I'd better ask the carving knife.* □ *Will your carving knife let you out to the pub tonight?*

carzey See carsey.

casher a trouser pocket containing cash. (Pickpockets' cant.) □ *Alf's out looking for cashers to lighten.* □ *People really don't take proper care of their cashers. It's almost too easy.*

cat and mouse a house. (Rhyming slang.) □ *That's a nice cat and mouse.* □ *Whose cat and mouse is that?*

cat's mother an insignificant female person. □ *I'm just the cat's mother, eh?* □ *Who do you think I am? The cat's mother?*

Cave! Look out! (Juvenile. From the Latin *cave*, meaning "beware.") □ *Cave! Here comes the teacher!* □ *He shouted "Cave!" but too late. The policeman saw what happened.*

century one hundred pounds sterling. (Underworld.) □ *I got a couple of centuries for driving these guys home from the bank.* □ *Here's a century for your trouble, young man.*

cert a certainty. □ *Oh yes, she's a dead cert all right.* □ *How do you know she's a cert?*

cessy foul; disgusting. □ *If you must be cessy, do so somewhere else thank you.* □ *That's really cessy, don't go in there.*

chain and locket a pocket. (Rhyming slang.) □ *Get yer hand out of yer chain and locket, son.* □ *Any change in your chain and locket?*

the **Chalfonts** haemorrhoids. (Rhyming slang, linked as follows: [the] Chalfonts = [Chalfont St Giles] ≈ [piles] = haemorrhoids. Chalfont St Giles is one of a group of villages in an area of

Buckinghamshire, near London, known collectively as the Chalfonts.) □ *Our Bert suffers terribly from the Chalfonts, you know.* □ *A bad dose of the Chalfonts is sheer hell.*

chalk and cheese diametric opposites. □ *I've never seen two people who were more like chalk and cheese.* □ *These two choices really are like chalk and cheese.*

chalkie a schoolteacher. □ *We got a new chalkie at school today.* □ *The chalkie told the children not to do that.*

champion excellent. □ *Your news is really champion, you know.* □ *What a champion idea that was.*

channel fleet a street. (Rhyming slang.) □ *There he was, walking down the channel fleet.* □ *She stood on the channel fleet and cried.*

chappie a man or boy. (A diminutive form of *chap*.) □ *Ask these chappies what they want.* □ *I say you chappie, what's up?*

charlie 1. a fool. □ *How can you be such a charlie?* □ *That poor charlie thinks he can convince them.* **2.** a night watchman. □ *Otto reckons the charlie'll be no problem.* □ *What do we do about the charlie if he tries to set off the alarm?*

charming wife a knife. (Rhyming slang.) □ *What are you carrying that charming wife for?* □ *Bring your charming wife over here and cut this loose.*

chartered libertine a person who does whatever he or she likes. □ *Here was one chartered libertine that was different from the others, he thought.* □ *I don't think I could take another chartered libertine like that today.*

chat a manner of speaking; a way of using language. □ *I don't think I like that sort of chat, okay?* □ *Oh, that's just chat for "difficult."*

chat someone up to talk informally to someone, with an ulterior motive. □ *I think I'll try chatting her up.* □ *He chatted up the girl, and then they left together.*

the **chattering classes** certain verbose members of the middle classes. □ *Most members of the chattering classes appear to be of a liberal disposition and often of a pretentiously artistic bias.* □ *How come the chattering classes seem to have a chartered right to appear on the television?*

cheerio AND **cheers 1.** a toast made upon drinking. □ *Cheers, and thanks.* □ *Well, cheerio! Good luck!* **2.** good wishes upon arriv-

ing or departing. □ *Cheerio, see you Monday.* □ *So long. Cheers.*
3. an expression of thanks. □ *That's helpful. Cheerio.* □ *Cheers.*
That's very handy.

cheers See cheerio.

cheesed off See browned off.

cheese-paring excessively economical. □ *What a miserable, cheese-paring affair it was.* □ *You could not be more cheese-paring if you tried, could you?*

cheeser a person with smelly feet. □ *Cor! He's a right cheeser!* □ *I can't stand cheesers.*

the **cherries** greyhound racing. (Rhyming slang, linked as follows: cherry [hogs] ≈ [dogs] = greyhound racing.) □ *He spent all his money on the cherries, and now he's broke.* □ *I'm off to the cherries tomorrow. Wish me luck!*

cherry ace a face. (Rhyming slang.) □ *His cherry ace was hidden behind a long white beard.* □ *I know that cherry ace. Who is he?*

cherry-ripe nonsense. (Rhyming slang, linked as follows: cherry ripe ≈ [tripe] = nonsense.) □ *What cherry-ripe that is!* □ *You're talking cherry-ripe again—as usual.*

chilled magnificent; fabulous. □ *Your pad is not what I'd call chilled, but it's certainly all right.* □ *What a chilled stereo that is!*

china a friend. (Rhyming slang, linked as follows: china [plate] ≈ [mate] = friend.) □ *Hello there, china!* □ *Of course Bert's my china.*

Chin-chin! **1.** a toast made upon drinking. □ *Chin-chin, and thanks!* □ *Well, chin-chin! Good luck!* **2.** good wishes upon arriving or departing. □ *Well, chin-chin Charlie, I hope all goes well!* □ *Chin-chin! What a lovely morning.*

chinless wonder a foolish upper-class person, usually male. □ *That chinless wonder thinks he can convince them.* □ *Sorry, he's still a genuine chinless wonder.*

chin someone to hit someone. □ *He chinned me as I walked over to my car.* □ *Harry's livid and out to chin you for what you did.*

chip to indulge in banter. □ *Oh, you're just chipping again!* □ *Would I chip with you, Mavis?*

chip butty a buttered bread roll sandwich filled with French fried potatoes. (North.) □ *A chip butty consists of a double helping of* *carbohydrate, with added grease. Healthy eating this is not. □ But on the other hand, a chip butty tastes great, especially when you're ravenous!*

chippery banter. □ *We just had some pleasant chippery after you left.* □ *What's all this chippery about?*

chippy 1. a fish and chip shop. □ *Fancy something from the chippy tonight, love?* □ *I'm just off down to the chippy.* **2.** resentful and arrogant in an irritating way. □ *Why do you always have to be so chippy?* □ *If you were less chippy you'd get more done.* **3.** AND **chips** a carpenter or joiner. (Also a term of address.) □ *Tell our chippy to come up here and put in a new floorboard.* □ *Tell me, chips, how fast can you build a coffin?*

chips See chippy.

chivvy someone AND **hassle someone** to harass someone; to bother someone; to give someone a difficult time. □ *Listen, please don't chivvy me. I've had a hard day.* □ *Please get this woman to stop hassling me!*

chiz a swindle or cheat. □ *What a chiz! I'm calling the police.* □ *I lost a fortune in that share chiz.*

chocker disgusted, fed up, or near to tears. □ *I'm chocker, really chocker!* □ *Fed up? I'm chocker!*

chock-full See bung-full.

chock up to cram in or make completely full. □ *Come on, we can really chock up this bin.* □ *Why has this cupboard been chocked up like this?*

chocolate box(y) [of popular art, particularly paintings] excessively sentimental or trashily pretentious. □ *This stuff is too chocolate boxy for me.* □ *A lot of people like chocolate box art.*

chokey prison. □ *"Welcome to your local chokey," said the warder.* □ *He knew he was going to end up in chokey.*

chop and change to vacillate. □ *Please don't keep chopping and changing, but just decide once and for all.* □ *Why must you always chop and change?*

chopper 1. a helicopter. □ *That chopper that reports on the traffic for the radio goes over my house every morning at 6 a.m.* □ *I never want to fly in a chopper. Those things scare me.* **2.** a tail. □ *Happy?*

He was as pleased as a dog with two choppers, I tell you. □ *Tell your kid to stop pulling on my cat's chopper.*

chop someone to hang; to execute. □ *We just heard. He's to be chopped.* □ *They will chop him all right.*

chucker-out(er) a strong man hired to eject unruly people from a bar or similar place. □ *He was the biggest chucker-outer I've ever seen.* □ *I saw the chucker-out looking at me, and I got out of there fast.*

Chuck it! Cease!; Stop it!; Give up! □ *Oh come on! Chuck it!* □ *Chuck it! That's enough!*

chuck it in AND **chuck one's hand in 1.** to quit; to give up; to cease trying. □ *I was so depressed, I almost chucked it in.* □ *If I didn't have to keep the job to live, I'd have chucked my hand in long ago.* **2.** to die. □ *The parrot chucked it in before I got it home.* □ *I was afraid I'd end up chucking my hand in.*

chuck one's hand in See chuck it in.

chuff 1. the buttocks. □ *Get off your chuff and on with your work!* □ *Still, it was funny when she fell on the mud and landed on her chuff.* **2.** an anal release of intestinal gas; a noise or smell associated with this. (Crude.) □ *The trouble with Joe is that he lets go of these chuffs all the time.* □ *I've told you before Joe—no more of these chuffs.*

chuffed 1. satisfied or delighted. (See also **dead chuffed.**) □ *I'm pleased you're chuffed. Don't get too chuffed yet.* **2.** flattered. □ *She appeared really chuffed at the compliment.* □ *I really wanted to deflate that silly chuffed fool.*

chump 1. the head. □ *Turn your chump around and take a look at this.* □ *He's distinctive because he has a particularly large chump.* **2.** a stupid person; a gullible person. □ *You are such a chump.* □ *See if that chump will loan you some money.*

the **Chunnel** a popular name for the Channel Tunnel. □ *We travelled to France through the Chunnel.* □ *Without doubt, the Chunnel is the best way to get across in bad weather.*

chunter (on) to grumble; to speak inarticulately. □ *Please don't chunter like that. Come right out with it!* □ *Why must you always chunter on?*

cig See ciggy.

ciggie See ciggy.

ciggy AND **cig; ciggie** a cigarette. □ *How about a ciggy before we take off?* □ *Where is my packet of ciggies?*

circs circumstances. □ *Whatever the circs, I won't do that.* □ *The circs better be very special before I could forgive that.*

the Circus a nickname for the British secret service. □ *Were you ever in the Circus?* □ *It's for you to discover who was and was not in the Circus.*

clack (on) to chatter at length. □ *She does clack on, doesn't she?* □ *Look, just stop clacking. OK?*

clag a cloud. □ *There's not a clag in the sky!* □ *Here comes a clag, full of nice wet rain.*

claggy [of clothes] wet and uncomfortable. □ *I hate this dress. It's so claggy.* □ *I must get out of these claggy clothes.*

clanger a blunder. □ *So I made a clanger! I wish you'd stop going on about it!* □ *Rubbing my nose in it is not going to correct the clanger.*

clapped out 1. [of people] tired or worn out. □ *Why are you always so clapped out?* □ *I am clapped out today.* **2.** [of equipment] worn out or broken. □ *There's your problem: a clapped out lynch pin.* □ *Is that clapped out car of yours still working?*

(clap)trap the mouth. □ *How do we get her claptrap closed so the rest can talk?* □ *Why don't you just shut your trap for a moment and listen?*

claret blood. □ *The sight of all that claret would make me sick.* □ *I discovered that Otto gets squeamish at the sight of claret, too!*

clatter someone to hit someone. □ *Fred got clattered, and that really made him angry.* □ *Tom clattered Fred on the hooter.*

claw-hammer suit AND **penguin suit** a man's formal evening suit, complete with tails. □ *There he stood, in his claw-hammer suit. What a laugh!* □ *Do I have to wear this ridiculous penguin suit, Mavis?*

clean bowl someone to bowl out or dismiss a batsman by directly hitting the wicket, without first touching either the bat or the player's body. (Cricket.) □ *Harris has never been clean bowled by anyone ever.* □ *Well, someone clean bowled him that time!*

clever nice; pleasant. (Usually employed in the negative.) □ *Well, I don't think that was so clever. I won't be going back to that hotel again.* □ *The weather's not too clever today.*

clever clogs AND **clever dick** someone who gives the impression of knowing everything; a smugly clever person; a know-all; a smart alec. □ *That clever clogs isn't of much use to our committee.* □ *Pete is such a clever dick!*

clever dick See clever clogs.

clever Mike a bicycle. (Rhyming slang, linked as follows: clever Mike ≈ [bike] = bicycle.) □ *What do you want with a clever Mike like that?* □ *I'm rather chuffed with my new clever Mike.*

click 1. a kilometre. □ *A click is about five eighths of a mile.* □ *We've got about ten more click to go.* **2.** [for a woman] to become pregnant. □ *I hear Sally has clicked.* □ *When I clicked, I wondered what to do.* **3.** to succeed; to have good luck. □ *Everything just clicked!* □ *Sometimes it clicks and it's great!*

clippie a bus conductress. □ *When I was young, I worked as a clippie.* □ *They were called clippies from their propensity to clip passengers' tickets.*

cloakroom a toilet. (A euphemism. Also literal.) □ *Where's the cloakroom?* □ *The cloakroom is through here.*

cloaks a cloakroom. □ *The cloaks is through that way.* □ *He hung his coat up in the cloaks, I think.*

clobber personal clothes or possessions. □ *I've lost all my clobber!* □ *What's all that clobber doing lying around here?*

clobber up to dress smartly. □ *We all got clobbered up before the party.* □ *Oh good, I like clobbering up.*

clock 1. a face. □ *The woman had a very unusual clock, you know.* □ *Why are you looking at me like that? Is there something wrong with my clock?* **2.** the period of 36 hours following cautioning and arrest of a suspect by the police. (Police slang. This is the maximum time a suspect can be held by the police without being charged and brought before a magistrate.) □ *We've got to charge him or let him go inside the clock, y'know.* □ *Clock has already started for Smith.*

clock someone 1. to hit someone, especially on the face. □ *He just clocked me, constable.* □ *Did you clock this gentleman, sir?* **2.** to

35

look at someone in an aggressive and threatening manner. □ *Don't clock me!* □ *Why are you clocking him like that?* **3.** to see or recognise someone. □ *Just then I thought I clocked someone in the crowd.* □ *He clocked me! He did!*

clodhopper a policeman. (Rhyming slang, linked as follows: clod-hopper ≈ [copper] = policeman.) □ *The clodhoppers are here looking for you again, Joe.* □ *What have you been doing to interest the clodhoppers this time?*

clogger a soccer player who regularly injures other players. □ *Watch that one over there. They say he's a clogger.* □ *Who was that great big clogger they had on their team?*

close to the knuckle AND **near (to) the knuckle** almost inde-cent. (This is hyphenated before a nominal.) □ *That dress of hers was, well, a bit close to the knuckle.* □ *Another one of your near-the-knuckle jokes again eh, Albert?*

clot a fool or blockhead. □ *You clot! You've buttered the tablecloth!* □ *Who's the clot in the bright orange trousers?*

cloth-eared AND **wooden-eared 1.** not listening; not prepared to listen. □ *Oh, she's only cloth-eared when it suits her.* □ *For once don't be so cloth-eared and listen to what I have to say!* **2.** partially deaf. □ *You don't have to shout. I'm not cloth-eared, you know.* □ *Just listen, you wooden-eared old sod!*

cloth ears AND **wooden ears 1.** one who does not or will not lis-ten. □ *I hate cloth ears who only hear what they want to hear.* □ *Don't be a wooden ears. Listen!* **2.** someone who is partially deaf. □ *Susan's a cloth ears. . . . I said, Susan is a cloth ears!* □ *How can a wooden ears hear what people are saying?*

clothes-peg an egg. (Rhyming slang.) □ *How much for a dozen clothes-pegs, love?* □ *Did you remember to get the clothes-pegs, Harry?*

clued up alert; knowledgeable. □ *If he says so, it's so. He's pretty clued up, you know.* □ *Ask Harry. He's usually clued up.*

coal and coke broke. (Rhyming slang.) □ *Tom's coal and coke. He'll have to go home.* □ *I'm coal and coke. Not a penny left.*

cock and hen ten pounds sterling. (Rhyming slang.) □ *These things cost more than just a few cock and hen, you know!* □ *Have you got a cock and hen you can spare me?*

cock-broth chicken soup. □ *Fancy a bowl of cock-broth?* □ *There's nothing better than some cock-broth on a cold day.*

cock(er) a male companion or friend. □ *Who's your cock, Albert?* □ *The two cockers left the pub, each one preventing the other from falling over.*

cock something up to make a mess of something. □ *If you must cock something up, try to make it something that doesn't matter.* □ *Why must you cock everything up?*

cock-sparrow a barrow. (Rhyming slang.) □ *The cock-sparrow was loaded down with fresh fruit.* □ *A man passed by, pushing a cock-sparrow.*

cock that won't fight a plan or proposal that cannot work. □ *That's a cock that won't fight. Forget it.* □ *Your cock that won't fight has just been approved by the board.*

cod a trick, hoax, or parody. □ *Don't you try to fool me with a cod like that!* □ *That was a really, really dumb cod!*

cod roe money. (Rhyming slang, linked as follows: cod roe ≈ [dough] = money. Compare with **bread**.) □ *It takes a lot of cod roe to buy a car like that.* □ *I don't make enough cod roe to go on a trip like that!*

cod's wallop See codswallop.

codswallop AND **cod's wallop** utter nonsense. □ *Boy, he can certainly churn out codswallop by the ton!* □ *That's just a lot of cod's wallop. Ignore it.*

cog a gear (on a car, etc.). □ *Don't crash the cogs!* □ *There's something wrong, I can't change cog.*

cog box a gear box. □ *Me car needs a new cog box.* □ *What's wrong? Cog box gone?*

coin it (in) to make vast sums of money rapidly. □ *If we advertise, we can coin it in.* □ *The promoter is coining it on this product.*

cold-meat job a case involving a corpse. (Police.) □ *There's a cold-meat job in Watson Street, Inspector.* □ *He's on his way to the cold-meat job right now.*

collect a gong to win a medal. □ *He goes to the Palace next week to collect a gong.* □ *Collecting a gong was not the most important objective of my career, you know.*

collins a letter thanking the host or hostess upon returning from a visit. (From a character in Jane Austen's novel *Pride and Prejudice*.) □ *I must write a collins to Mrs Jackson to thank her for last night's wonderful dinner party.* □ *Well, that's nice. Only Mrs Harris has had the courtesy to send a collins.*

come a clover to fall over. □ *I came a clover on a flagstone outside my house.* □ *Don't come a clover!*

come back to repeat what one has just said. □ *Why are you coming back again?* □ *Please stop coming back on yourself over and over again.*

come it to behave aggressively or presumptuously. □ *Don't you come it with me!* □ *He tried to come it but I got the better of him.*

come over queer to feel ill suddenly. □ *Mary came over queer and had to go home.* □ *If you come over queer like that again, I want to know.*

come the innocent to pretend innocence. □ *Don't you come the innocent with me, my lad!* □ *He's coming the innocent, but we'll get to the truth.*

come the old soldier with someone 1. to wheedle, importune, or take liberties with someone. □ *Don't you come the old soldier with me!* □ *He tried to come the old soldier with us, but we disabused him of that in short order.* **2.** to dominate or impose one's own views upon someone, by virtue of presumed superior knowledge or experience. □ *Don't come the old soldier with me. I know better than that.* □ *Although he tried to come the old soldier with the doctor, he got nowhere.*

come to a sticky end to be murdered; to die in some particularly gory way. □ *If you go on like that you'll come to a sticky end.* □ *I knew he'd come to a sticky end.*

come to the wrong shop to ask something in the wrong place. □ *Woops! I've come to the wrong shop, haven't I?* □ *This is the vet's surgery. If you want your toothache attended to, you've come to the wrong shop.*

come under the hammer to auction (something). □ *The house at the corner is coming under the hammer next week.* □ *What's come under the hammer this week, then?*

common (dog) common sense. □ *Anyone with an ounce of common dog should be able to do that, Otto.* □ *The problem with common is that it's not common at all.*

common or garden normal or usual. □ *Oh, that's just the common or garden kind.* □ *Really, any old common or garden one will do.*

conchie a conscientious objector. □ *Otto was a conchie in the war, you know.* □ *Otto? The only things he was ever a conchie about were hard work and honest effort.*

congratters congratulations. □ *Congratters! Well done.* □ *Just to say congratters on your new baby.*

conk AND **konk 1.** a large or particularly obtrusive nose. □ *Have you seen the size of that guy's conk?* □ *Joan bonked Pete on his big red konk.* **2.** the head. □ *Harry's distinctive hairy conk hove into view.* □ *Where'd you get that nasty bump on your konk?*

constant screamer a concertina. (Rhyming slang.) □ *My uncle used to play the constant screamer, and everyone would dance.* □ *Constant screamers are kinda rare nowadays.*

constipated reluctant to part with money. □ *When it comes to handing out money, she's as constipated as they get.* □ *Come on, you constipated old miser. It's a good cause.*

conversion job a heavy beating. □ *After a conversion job like that, the guy spent two weeks in the hospital.* □ *Bruno gave the guy a terrible conversion job.*

coo AND **cor** God. (A euphemism and disguise.) □ *Coo, she's a real looker!* □ *Cor, what's young Alf done now?*

cook See Captain Cook.

cooking busy. □ *The phone was cooking for more than an hour.* □ *I was cooking and couldn't get to the phone.*

cop a packet AND **get a packet** to become badly injured; to be wounded severely. (Originally military.) □ *Me uncle copped a packet in Normandy.* □ *If you want to get a packet or worse, just stand up in that shallow trench, son.*

cop it 1. to be found out; to be caught. □ *He copped it right in the middle of the attack, sir.* □ *If they try that here they'll cop it for sure.* **2.** to be made to endure; to be punished. □ *You're just going to have to cop it until we get this sorted.* □ *You'll cop it for that* *behaviour, I promise.* **3.** to become pregnant. □ *Has she copped it again?* □ *Zoe has been trying to cop it for months, you know.*

cop (on to) something to understand or become aware of something. □ *I think I'm copping on to the significance of this at last.* □ *Try to cop what I'm saying, Otto.*

cop someone to arrest someone. □ *The police copped Jed for speeding.* □ *I was copped for doing absolutely nothing at all.*

cor See coo.

corblimey See blimey.

Corgi and Bess the annual television broadcast made by Queen Elizabeth on Christmas Day. (Her pet corgi dogs are usually in evidence. The phrase is a play on *Porgy and Bess*, which is the title of an opera by George and Ira Gershwin.) □ *What do we call a Corgi and Bess if the corgis don't turn up?* □ *Corgi and Bess is the highlight of Christmas Day for Aunt Mary.*

corned beef a thief. (Rhyming slang.) □ *We are the police. We are here to catch a corned beef, madam.* □ *This little tramp is just another corned beef.*

Cornish (pasty) 1. a pastry turnover containing seasoned meats and vegetables. □ *Alfred has a Cornish pasty every day for lunch.* □ *I like the occasional Cornish, too.* **2.** a wide, thickly soled heavy-duty man's shoe. □ *A lot of the older working men around here still wear Cornish pasties.* □ *The Cornish was a practical solution to a practical pedestrian problem.*

cosh 1. a bludgeon or blackjack. □ *"All right son, why are you carrying a cosh?" the policeman asked him.* □ *He took out a cosh and threatened me.* **2.** to bludgeon. □ *He tried to cosh me but I managed to run off.* □ *Have you ever been coshed?*

cost a packet AND **cost the earth** to be very expensive or costly. □ *It'll cost a packet to do that.* □ *I don't care if that painting costs the earth. Buy it!*

cost the earth See cost a packet.

cottaging the habit of spending the weekend at a second home in the country. □ *We go cottaging in Suffolk most weekends.* □ *This area is full of houses belonging to people who do a lot of cottaging.*

cotton wool on top unburdened with excessive intelligence. □ *She's, well, rather cotton wool on top, you know.* □ *We do not need any more of these cotton wool on top people in here.*

cough 1. to confess to a crime. (Police.) □ *Are you going to cough?* □ *All right, all right. I'll cough to the break-in but not the assault.* **2.** useful or general information. (Police.) □ *Here's some cough you might find handy.* □ *Well, that is useful cough!*

cough and stutter AND **mutter and stutter** butter. (Rhyming slang.) □ *I like cough and stutter on me bread. Don't you?* □ *Half a pound of mutter and stutter, please.*

country cousin a dozen. (Rhyming slang.) □ Q: *How many eggs?* A: *A country cousin, please.* □ *There's about a country cousin of people here to see you, Claire.*

a **couple of bob** a small, non-specific sum of money. (Literally, two shillings in old currency or ten pence in new currency. *Bob* was a slang term for a shilling.) □ *I'm afraid there is not even a couple of bob left in that account.* □ *Of course I can afford it. It's just a couple of bob.*

Cousin Jack a Cornishman, especially a tin miner. □ *Ivor's a Cousin Jack. He comes from Penzance.* □ *What have you got against Cousin Jacks?*

the **Cousins** Americans; the U.S. government; the United States. (A term used in British government circles rather than among the general public. It is not necessarily meant in a complimentary way.) □ *Do we know what the Cousins really want?* □ *We never know what the Cousins are really after.*

cover in to cover or roof over. □ *We have to cover in this trench before nightfall.* □ *Why did you cover in the box, Jean?*

cow and calf 1. a half. (Rhyming slang.) □ *Surely a cow and calf's enough.* □ *It's just a cow and calf, but I want it all.* **2.** one pound and fifty pence; formerly, thirty shillings. (Rhyming slang, linked as follows: cow and calf ≈ half [of one pound sterling].) □ *That'll be a cow and calf, missus.* □ *He wanted me to pay a cow and calf for this worthless thing!*

cowhorns tall curved handles upon a bicycle or motorcycle. □ *Are you sure these cowhorns are safe?* □ *I just love riding it with these cowhorns.*

cozzer AND **cozzpot** a policeman. □ *See that cozzer over there? He lifted me once.* □ *The cozzpots will catch up with you some day.*

cozzpot See cozzer.

crack on to talk endlessly. □ *Oh, he'll crack on till doomsday.* □ *The old friends cracked on for ages about old memories and old friends.*

crack one's face to smile. □ *Try cracking your face, just for once.* □ *Come on, now. Crack your face.*

crasher See crashing bore.

crashing bore AND **crasher; crusher** an exceptionally tedious or boring person or thing. □ *I don't think I could take another crashing bore like that today.* □ *One crusher was no different from the others, he thought.*

crawling with it exceptionally wealthy. □ *There are not many people crawling with it like him.* □ *Ken is crawling with it because of the money his uncle left him.*

creaking gate an invalid who neither recovers nor gets worse. □ *It's terrible—she's been a creaking gate for months now and we don't know what to do.* □ *I hope I'm never a creaking gate like that.*

creased exhausted; unable to continue. □ *I feel too creased to go to work today.* □ *Poor Ted really looks creased.*

crem a crematorium. □ *Aunt Mavis's funeral was at the crem.* □ *That's the crem, where Aunt Mavis is now.*

crib 1. to plagiarise. □ *Smith! You cribbed these answers, didn't you?* □ *I didn't crib nuffink, sir.* **2.** to grumble; to complain. □ *Why do you always have to crib?* □ *There he is, cribbing as usual.* **3.** an aid to cheating in an examination, such as written notes. □ *I'm afraid there's no doubt that Smith took a crib into the examination with him, headmaster.* □ *If I had a crib, where is it then, sir?*

crikey AND **cripes; cringe; crumbs** Christ. (A euphemism and disguise. Crude.) □ *Crikey, I hope we get there on time.* □ *Well crumbs, I didn't think it mattered so much.*

crimper a hairdresser. □ *Would you ever guess that Bert was once a ladies' crimper?* □ *The crimper looked like a right poof.*

cringe See crikey.

cringe someone to embarrass someone. □ *Why did you have to cringe me like that?* □ *He really cringed him.*

crinkle See crinkly.

crinkly 1. AND **crumblie** a senile or very old person. (Offensive. Also a term of address.) □ *Take care where the crinklies are crossing the road.* □ *Just remember we'll each of us be a crumblie ourselves one day, with luck.* **2.** AND **crinkle** a banknote; paper money. □ *That'll be 15 please, sir. Or 10 in crinkles, if you like.* □ *How much crinkle do you need, then?* □ *Sorry, I can't afford it. I've no crinkly.*

cripes See crikey.

crisp to die by arson. □ *I really would hate to be crisped in a fire. What a way to go.* □ *Three people crisped in that big fire last night.*

criss-cross a crossword puzzle. □ *I like to complete the criss-cross every morning while having my breakfast.* □ *I don't enjoy criss-crosses.*

crowie an old woman. □ *Ask the crowie what she wants, please.* □ *There's a crowie here asking for you.*

crucial excellent; wonderful. □ *What a crucial idea that was.* □ *Your news is really crucial, you know.*

crumblie See crinkly.

crumbs See crikey.

crusher 1. a policeman. □ *The crusher broke up the fight.* □ *These two crushers drove around in their car picking on innocent people like me.* **2.** See crashing bore.

crust the head. □ *Where'd you get that nasty bump on your crust?* □ *Harry's distinctive hairy crust hove into view.*

cry stinking fish to belittle or disparage one's own efforts or the efforts of one's family, friends, or fellow workers. □ *Do you have to go around crying stinking fish?* □ *To cry stinking fish is not a good way to be popular with the people closest to you.*

cuddle and kiss a girl. (Rhyming slang, linked as follows: cuddle and kiss ≈ [miss] = girl.) □ *Jack's round at his cuddle and kiss.* □ *So this cuddle and kiss asks what I thought of the international situation!*

cuppa a cup of tea. (Compare with muggo.) □ *I sat down and had a lovely cuppa.* □ *A cuppa is always welcome.*

currant bun 1. a son. (Rhyming slang.) □ *That's Mr Big's currant bun, you know.* □ *He stood there with his currant bun.* **2.** the sun.

(Rhyming slang.) □ *The currant bun was shining bright, high in the sky.* □ *The light from the currant bun was right in his eyes.* **3. Currant Bun** the *Sun.* (Rhyming slang. The *Sun* is a daily newspaper.) □ *I once tried to read the Currant Bun but couldn't find anything much more than pictures to look at.* □ *My next-door neighbour reads the Currant Bun every day.* **4.** (on) the run. (Rhyming slang. Refers to running from the police, etc.) □ *Otto's on the currant bun again.* □ *Going currant bun won't help. They'll still find you, sooner or later.*

curtain climber a young child. □ *I wish she would try to control that curtain climber of hers.* □ *I hope you like curtain climbers. There are several here this afternoon.*

cushy 1. soft; easy. (From *cushion.*) □ *He's got sort of a cushy job.* □ *That's a cushy kind of life to lead.* **2.** safe. □ *Oh, you're cushy there. No one will notice.* □ *Is there somewhere cushy around here where I'll be all right?*

custard and jelly television. (Rhyming slang, linked as follows: custard and jelly ≈ [telly] = television.) □ *He watched the custard and jelly all day long.* □ *I try to get through the day without watching any custard and jelly.*

cut along to depart. □ *All right, cut along now Smith.* □ *The teacher told me to cut along, sir.*

cut up rough to exhibit resentment, bad temper, or anger. □ *Otto really cut up rough when he was told.* □ *Don't cut up rough or you'll get fired.*

dab hand an expert; a skilled amateur. □ *Jim's a dab hand with computers.* □ *No one could ever call me a dab hand at this sort of thing.*

dabs AND **darbies** fingerprints. □ *They found a good set of dabs on the window.* □ *Why did they want my darbies?*

daffy-headed lacking intelligence. □ *I think you could say he's, well, sort of daffy-headed.* □ *Who's that daffy-headed clown in there?*

daily 1. a cleaning woman visiting daily. □ *Why is our daily walking through our office in the middle of the day?* □ *I know we have a daily but I'm afraid I've never seen her.* **2. Daily** See Daily Mail.

Daily (Mail) 1. a story, especially a hard-luck story. (Rhyming slang, linked as follows: Daily (Mail) ≈ [tale] = story. The *Daily Mail* is a newspaper published in London.) □ *I listened to his Daily Mail and gave him five quid.* □ *It's certainly a very sad Daily. In fact, it's almost a pity he made it all up.* **2.** the buttocks. (Rhyming slang, linked as follows: Daily (Mail) ≈ [tail] = buttocks.) □ *She fell right on her Daily Mail.* □ *There is some mustard or something on your Daily.* **3.** court bail. (Rhyming slang, linked as follows: Daily (Mail) ≈ bail.) □ *I don't know how he ever got Daily Mail.* □ *I'd never give him Daily, not ever!* **4.** beer. (Rhyming slang, linked as follows: Daily (Mail) ≈ [ale] = beer.) □ *Can I have Daily Mail please?* □ *I do like this Daily they have in here.* **5.** a nail. (The kind that gets hammered into wood, etc. Rhyming slang, linked as follows: Daily (Mail) ≈ nail.) □ *He hammered at the Daily Mail, but it would not go in.* □ *Pass the Dailies, mate.* **6.** a fingernail. (Rhyming slang, linked as follows: Daily (Mail) ≈ [nail] = fingernail.) □ *Oh look, I've split me Daily Mail!* □ *How did you do that to yer Daily?* **7.** the post. (Rhyming slang, linked as follows: Daily (Mail) ≈ [mail] = post.) □ *Anything in the Daily Mail for me today?* □ *The postman handed her her Daily.*

daisy-cutter 1. a perfect landing by an aircraft. □ *This boy's a good pilot. Look, another daisy-cutter!* □ *He made a daisy-cutter and taxied to the terminal.* **2.** a cricket ball that fails to rise when it is delivered. □ *Watch out for these daisy-cutters.* □ *A daisy-cutter is sneaky because it gets under the defences, as it were.*

daisy roots boots. (Rhyming slang.) □ *Why are you in your daisy roots? Is it muddy out?* □ *I find these daisy roots uncomfortable.*

damager a manager. □ *Have you seen our new damager yet? I'll give him a week!* □ *Damager? Yeh, that's about the right name for him.*

damn all absolutely nothing. (Crude.) □ *I have damn all to do these days.* □ *I assure you, there is damn all here!*

danny an unmarked police car. □ *Watch it! That's a danny!* □ *The danny drove forward, blocking my exit.*

darbies 1. hands. (Rhyming slang, linked as follows: darbie ≈ [Derby Band] = hand. A Derby Band was a bond made to a moneylender in 17th-century London. *Derby* is pronounced "DAR-by." Always in the plural.) □ *Show me yer darbies, son. What 'ave you been doing to get 'em so mucky?* □ *He grabbed me by the darbies and told me to do what he said.* **2.** handcuffs. (Rhyming slang, linked as follows: darbie ≈ [Derby Band] = handcuff. Always in the plural.) □ *The constable slipped the darbies on me as quick as get out.* □ *My hands were locked together behind my back in his darbies, and I felt a kind of claustrophobia coming over me.* **3.** See **dabs**.

Darby and Joan 1. a long and happily married elderly couple. □ *Are they not a lovely Darby and Joan?* □ *Do you think we will be a Darby and Joan one day?* **2.** a telephone. (Rhyming slang, linked as follows: Darby and Joan ≈ (tele)phone.) □ *You'll find a Darby and Joan over in that corner.* □ *He's got one of them portable Darby and Joans.*

Darby and Joan club an old age pensioners' club. □ *I think she spends more and more time at the Darby and Joan club.* □ *The Darby and Joan club is very popular with the old folks.*

dark blue 1. a present or former student of Harrow School. □ *All our family have been dark blues.* □ *The most famous dark blue was Sir Winston Churchill.* **2.** a present or former student of Oxford University. □ *George is a dark blue.* □ *If I were a dark blue, I would really appreciate my good fortune.*

dash 1. damn. (A euphemism and disguise.) □ *Oh dash, there's the turnoff.* □ *Where's the dashed cat?* **2.** money. □ *I don't make enough dash to go on a trip like that!* □ *It takes a lot of dash to buy a car like that.*

Dash it all! Oh, phooey!; To hell with it all! □ *Oh, dash it all! I'm late.* □ *I broke it! Dash it all!*

the **day after the fair** when it is too late. □ *Once more, you get here the day after the fair. How do you do it?* □ *He made his offer the day after the fair, I'm afraid. Just too late.*

day's a-dawning the morning. (Rhyming slang.) □ *Day's a-dawning, and bitter cold!* □ *Good night. See you in the day's a-dawning.*

dead-and-alive monotonous or boring. □ *I've never been in such a dead-and-alive place.* □ *Unexciting? It was dead-and-alive!*

dead cert an absolute certainty; an easy thing to do. □ *It's a dead cert. I foresee no problems.* □ *The job was not a dead cert, but we did it on time.*

dead chuffed AND **real chuffed** very satisfied or pleased. □ *He was dead chuffed to win.* □ *I'm real chuffed to win this!*

dead-end kid a youth with no future, usually a male. □ *Kelly wasn't your typical dead-end kid.* □ *Max was a dead-end kid from the day he was born.*

dead trouble very serious trouble. (Always with *in*.) □ *You're in dead trouble, my lad!* □ *I'll be in dead trouble if I get caught.*

debag to remove a man's trousers as a prank. □ *Philip got debagged at his stag party last night.* □ *I wish they wouldn't debag people.*

deb's delight an upper-class young man who is considered a socially acceptable marriage partner for the daughters of upper-class families. (*Deb* is an abbreviation of *debutante*.) □ *I think Basil is what they call a deb's delight.* □ *If that's a deb's delight, then I'm glad I'm not a deb.*

decider the round of a sport or game—often an additional one after a draw—that determines the victor. □ *I think this will have to go to a decider next week.* □ *Are you going to be at tonight's decider?*

dee-aitch the head. (Backslang.) □ Harry's distinctive hairy dee-aitch hove into view. □ Where'd you get that nasty bump on your dee-aitch?

deep-sea diver a five pound note. (Rhyming slang, linked as follows: deep-sea diver ≈ [fiver] = five pound note.) □ I'll take a deep-sea diver for my trouble, squire. □ It costs a few deep-sea divers to be driven home in a taxi.

deep-sea fisherman a card sharper on an ocean-going liner or cruise ship. □ That friendly old card partner you've found is a deep-sea fisherman, I'm sure. □ Deep-sea fishermen can make a lot of money out of the suckers they find on board.

deff out to lose contact with one's female friends after acquiring a steady boyfriend. (Teens.) □ Maureen had deffed out within a week of meeting Tony. □ I won't deff out on you like Maureen did, girls.

degree of frost the number of degrees below freezing. (Refers to the Fahrenheit system of temperature measurement, not the Celsius one.) □ There were ten degrees of frost last night. □ If there are thirty degrees of frost, that's really cold!

dekko a glance or quick look. □ Take a dekko at that! □ He took a quick dekko but saw nothing unusual.

derro a vagrant; someone who has fallen on really bad times. (An abbreviation of derelict.) □ By midnight the derros had gone wherever they go to sleep, and we got that part of town to ourselves. □ There are always a lot of derros hanging around that part of town.

derry a derelict building. □ That derry is dangerous, Tommy. Don't play near it. □ They're going to pull down the derry at last, I hear.

designer jury a jury "designed" by the careful use of challenges by defence lawyers. □ It will be interesting to see how this designer jury behaves. □ Some people think designer juries give an unfair advantage to the defence.

deuce 1. two pounds sterling. □ Can you lend me a deuce till payday? □ All right, here's a deuce. Don't spend it all in one shop. **2.** bad luck. (An old word for the Devil.) □ What rotten deuce. □ Once we've got the deuce behind us it must get better, right?

dial a face. □ I know that dial. Who is he? □ His dial was hidden behind a long white beard.

dib a partly smoked cigarette. □ *He produced a dib from his pocket and relit it.* □ *I threw my dib away and turned to look him in the eye.*

dibs and dabs body or pubic lice. (Taboo. Rhyming slang, linked as follows: dibs and dabs ≈ [crabs] = (body/pubic) lice.) □ *I'm afraid all of these refugees have dibs and dabs.* □ *The first thing is to check for dibs and dabs on everyone.*

dicker a lookout. □ *Otto, you're the dicker.* □ *Why am I always the dicker?*

dickory dock a clock. (Rhyming slang.) □ *The dickory dock in the kitchen has broken.* □ *Wind your dickory dock before you forget.*

dicky 1. unreliable; likely to collapse or to fail. □ *I'm afraid this car of mine's a bit dicky.* □ *He's got a dicky heart, you know.* **2.** unwell. □ *Carol is a bit dicky today, I'm afraid.* □ *Oh dear, I feel rather dicky.* **3.** See dicky dirt.

dicky bow a bow tie. □ *Tom's the one in the dicky bow.* □ *I like men who wear a dicky bow.*

dicky-diddle to urinate. (Crude. Rhyming slang, linked as follows: dicky-diddle ≈ [piddle] = urinate.) □ *I've got to dicky-diddle. Back in a minute.* □ *He just went out to dicky-diddle.*

dicky (dirt) a shirt. (Rhyming slang.) □ *Where's me dicky dirts, woman?* □ *Otto looked good in that colourful new dicky you got him.*

dicky seat 1. the driver's seat on a horse-drawn carriage. □ *He got up into the dicky seat and drove off.* □ *A new driver sat in the dicky seat that day.* **2.** an extra seat at the rear of a vehicle that folds away when not in use. □ *You don't see many dicky seats nowadays.* □ *There was once a dicky seat in almost every car.*

didn't oughter AND **dirty daughter** water. (Rhyming slang.) □ *A pitcher of didn't oughter had been placed on the table.* □ *I'm so thirsty! A drink of dirty daughter would be most welcome.*

dimmo an unintelligent person. □ *What's a dimmo like that doing around here?* □ *I'm sorry but we really don't need another dimmo working here.*

ding-dong 1. a song. (Rhyming slang.) □ *Oh yes, I love that old ding-dong.* □ *Now there's a ding-dong that brings back old memories, eh?* **2.** a fight; a quarrel. □ *That was some ding-dong last* *night.* □ *Who's going to win the ding-dong, I ask?* **3.** See **ding-dong bell**.

ding-dong (bell) hell. (Rhyming slang.) □ *What the ding-dong bell is going on here?* □ *It's as hot as ding-dong down here.*

dinghy a motorcycle sidecar. □ *You don't see many motorbikes with dinghies nowadays.* □ *Here he comes, with his girl in the dinghy.*

dip out 1. to be unlucky. □ *Trust me to dip out.* □ *When I dip out, I just pick myself up and try again.* **2.** to avoid or escape some duty or responsibility. □ *I know you tried to dip out. Don't try it again.* □ *We've got to dip out of this place.*

dirty daughter See **didn't oughter**.

dirty mac brigade lecherous old men as a group. □ *I think almost all the people watching the film were in the dirty mac brigade.* □ *Why do there seem to be so many members of the dirty mac brigade in this part of town?*

dirty weekend a weekend spent with one's lover rather than one's spouse. □ *I think they're off to Paris for a dirty weekend.* □ *Do people still go on dirty weekends?*

dischuffed dissatisfied; displeased. □ *I think it is important for you to know that I am dischuffed indeed by your performance.* □ *A dischuffed boss is a dangerous boss.*

dish someone out of something to be deprived of something by cheating. □ *He still considers himself dished out of promotion.* □ *Don't try to dish me out of that one, too!*

dishy attractive. (Usually sexually.) □ *Now that woman is really dishy!* □ *She certainly looks dishy to me!*

the Ditch the English Channel. □ *We stood there looking over the Ditch at France.* □ *We sailed to France across the Ditch.*

div a stupid old person. (Criminal.) □ *These divs are easy targets for all the small-time crooks around.* □ *Divs are just too tempting.*

dive bomber someone—such as a vagrant—who collects cigarette ends from the pavement with a view to smoking them. □ *It was a cold night and no one was to be seen but a lonely dive bomber slowly working her way along the street.* □ *We don't want dive bombers around here, they're bad for the image of our town.*

DJ a dinner jacket. □ *You'll be expected to wear a DJ at tonight's event.* □ *Everyone stood there in DJs—except me.*

do a beer AND **do a drink; do a drop; do a one** to take an alcoholic drink. □ *I'll do a beer, thanks.* □ *Do me a drop, too.*

do a Bertie to turn Queen's evidence in a criminal trial. (From a certain Bertie Small, who did this.) □ *Mick would never do a Bertie on you.* □ *Mike has done a Bertie.*

do a bunk AND **do a Michael; do a mick(e)y; do a runner** to depart rapidly, disappear, or escape. □ *He did a bunk before he was fired.* □ *Time for us all to do a runner, I think. They'll be home soon.*

do a drink See do a beer.

do a drop See do a beer.

do a flanker (on someone) AND **pull a flanker (on someone); work a flanker (on someone)** to trick, outwit, or deceive someone; to evade someone or something. □ *You can try to do a flanker on me if you like, but I'm on to your tricks.* □ *Don't try to work a flanker on me!* □ *I realised too late that John had pulled a flanker.*

do a Houdini to escape. (After the feats of the late Harry Houdini.) □ *There was no time to do a Houdini, so we had to talk to Mrs Wilson.* □ *Lefty tried to do a Houdini.*

do a Michael See do a bunk.

do a mick(e)y See do a bunk.

do a one See do a beer.

do a runner See do a bunk.

do a show to go to a theatrical entertainment. □ *We'll do a show while we're in London.* □ *I'd rather like to do a show, too.*

do a starry to sleep under the stars. □ *Other people would rather die than do a starry.* □ *Other people love doing a starry.*

do as you like a bicycle. (Rhyming slang, linked as follows: do as you like ≈ [bike] = bicycle.) □ *You have to wear a helmet with a do as you like that size, don't you?* □ *How much did that do as you like set you back?*

dob a small lump or dollop. □ *There was a dob of the stuff on the plate, but I wasn't going to eat it.* □ *All right, give me a dob.*

dock asthma theatrically expressed surprise or disbelief displayed by the accused in court. (Police and criminal slang.) □ *Terry's denial was interrupted by long gasps of dock asthma.* □ *It was the* *most convincing display of dock asthma the judge had seen for many a year.*

dodgy gear AND **dodgy kit** stolen goods. □ *All right, then tell us where this dodgy gear came from?* □ *We found a huge pile of dodgy kit in his house.*

dodgy kit See dodgy gear.

do for someone 1. to serve as housekeeper for someone. □ *She does for the elderly gent in the big house.* □ *I do for people because it makes some money for me.* **2.** to clean someone's house on a regular basis. □ *He has a woman who comes in every day to do for him.* □ *Mrs Wilson does for a couple of the old folks who have houses around here.* **3.** AND **do someone in** to kill someone. □ *That fellow did for his girl, you know.* □ *Someone had done in that poor old lady.*

dog and bone a telephone. (Rhyming slang, linked as follows: dog and bone ≈ (tele)phone.) □ *The dog and bone was ringing off the hook when I came in.* □ *The dog and bone's been very busy all day today.*

dog out to keep watch. □ *Bert, you go and dog out while we get on with things here.* □ *Instead of dogging out, Bert went and let the dog out, which barked and attracted attention.*

dog's breakfast AND **dog's dinner** a mess; a shambles. □ *What a dog's breakfast this place has become.* □ *Why do you have to make a dog's dinner of every place you live at?*

dog's dinner See dog's breakfast.

dollars AND **bucks** pounds sterling; money. □ *How many bucks does this thing cost?* □ *I don't have any dollars on me.*

dolly 1. pretty or attractive. □ *Norah really is quite dolly.* □ *That girl next door certainly is dolly!* **2.** a cricket ball that is easy to hit or catch. □ *Here comes a dolly for you, Charles!* □ *Oh, Charles! Missing a dolly!*

do me good 1. a cigarette. (Rhyming slang, linked as follows: do me good ≈ [Wood(bine)] = cigarette. "Woodbine" was a brand of cigarette especially popular with troops on the Western Front during World War I.) □ *Where is my packet of do me goods?* □ *How about a do me good before we take off?* **2.** wood. (Rhyming slang.) □ *We need more do me good to finish this job.* □ *There's a great pile of do me good in the garden next door.*

done over 1. beaten up; successfully assaulted. □ *We done over the other guys good and proper, and they knew it.* □ *Harry felt that Mike would get the idea if he was done over a bit.* **2.** frisked or searched. □ *He looked at his done over flat and sighed.* □ *Why were you done over? What were they looking for?*

the **done thing** the acceptable way of doing things. □ *This is the done thing.* □ *That is not the done thing.*

donkey's ages See donkey's years.

donkey's years AND **donkey's ages** a very long time. □ *I haven't seen you in donkey's years.* □ *It's been donkey's ages since we talked.*

don't care tuppence totally disinterested. □ *I don't care tuppence, really.* □ *Why should you worry? You don't care tuppence either.*

don't make a fuss a bus. (Rhyming slang.) □ *I saw him on the don't make a fuss this morning.* □ *Waiting for the don't make a fuss, eh?*

do one's fruit AND **do one's nut** to become furiously angry. □ *I'd do my fruit if that happened to me, I can tell you!* □ *Boss, there's a customer out here doing his nut.*

do one's nut See do one's fruit.

door to door a door. (Rhyming slang.) □ *He's at the old door to door.* □ *I knocked on yer door to door, but no one answered.*

dosh money. □ *Sorry, I can't afford it, I've no dosh.* □ *How much dosh do you need, then?*

do someone to arrest someone. □ *The rozzers tried to do Frank too, but he moved away too fast.* □ *The cops did her as she was leaving the hotel.*

do someone down to harm someone. □ *Don't do your family down like that.* □ *I'm sorry about your difficulty, but don't do me down because of that.*

do someone in See do for someone.

do someone up like a kipper to steal from someone by trickery; to cheat. □ *Oh we did the little creep up like a kipper all right, Martin.* □ *I keep being done up like a kipper by people who seem to see me as a soft target.*

dots sheet music. □ *Right, who's got the dots?* □ *You can buy the dots for this in that music shop in High Street.*

dot someone to hit or strike someone. □ *I got heavily dotted by Harry yesterday.* □ *Harry dotted him one right on the jaw.*

double bubble See bubble.

double-choked extremely disgusted. □ *Heavens, we were all double-choked, I think.* □ *I don't want to be double-choked again.*

down to the ground completely, utterly, or entirely. □ *He was fed up, right down to the ground.* □ *Why are you so rotten all the way down to the ground?*

downy shrewd or knowing. □ *He's a downy one all right. You won't fool him.* □ *We need a downy individual in that job.*

dozy lazy or stupid. □ *Who is that dozy fellow leaning on the bar?* □ *He may look dozy, but he knows what he's doing.*

draw the long bow to exaggerate. □ *I wish I could stop her drawing the long bow as she does.* □ *If you keep drawing the long bow, no one will believe anything you say.*

drinking token AND **beer token; drinking voucher; beer voucher** a one pound coin. □ *Have you got a few drinking tokens you can spare?* □ *These things cost more than just a beer voucher or two.*

drinking voucher See drinking token.

drink (money) 1. blackmail money. □ *I've got to pay them drink money or else!* □ *Gimme the drink you owe me!* 2. money paid by the police for information supplied. □ *If it's good information, you'll get your drink.* □ *How much drink money is this news worth?*

drop a clanger to commit a serious blunder. □ *Woops! I dropped a clanger there, didn't I?* □ *Try not to drop any more clangers, Ivan.*

drop (a pup) to give birth. □ *Samantha dropped a pup last week.* □ *When do you drop?*

drophead 1. a convertible car. □ *I'm rather partial to dropheads.* □ *Like my new drophead, darling?* 2. the removable fabric roof of a convertible car. □ *I only remove the drophead when there's no danger of rain.* □ *The drophead's not been off this car since it was new.*

drop off the twig See hop off (one's twig).

a drop of the hard stuff a drink of spirits. □ *Graham always liked a drop of the hard stuff.* □ *A drop of the hard stuff sounds tempting just now.*

dropped arrested. □ *Harry's just been dropped by the rozzers.* □ *If you want to be dropped, just keep on behaving like that.*

drown something to overdilute spirits by adding too much water. □ *Don't drown that perfectly good whisky!* □ *The English always drown the stuff.*

drum and fife **1.** a knife. (Rhyming slang.) □ *Swiftly and silently his drum and fife found its way up under Rocko's ribs.* □ *I could tell from the way his cuff broke that there was a drum and fife strapped to his leg.* **2.** a wife. (Rhyming slang.) □ *I've got to go home to my drum and fife.* □ *My drum and fife disapproved of the film.*

drummer **1.** a thief; a burglar. □ *This little vagrant is just another drummer.* □ *We are the police. We are here to catch drummers, madam.* **2.** a door-to-door salesman. □ *There's a drummer at the door.* □ *I tried being a drummer for a while but hated it.*

drumming thieving; burglary. □ *There's a lot of drumming in this area.* □ *He was actually doing a drumming when we arrested him, sarge.*

drum up to make tea by the side of the road. □ *A couple of tramps were drumming up in the lay-by.* □ *This would be a good place to drum up.*

dry old stick an old man with a dry sense of humour. □ *There's some dry old stick here looking for you.* □ *The dry old stick sat on the bench and told a series of very funny stories.*

dry-shave to delude someone. □ *Don't let him dry-shave you.* □ *The scoundrel dry-shaved me!*

dub out See dub up.

dub someone up to incarcerate or jail someone. □ *Don't let them dub me up!* □ *They dub people up for that sort of thing, you know.*

dub up AND **dub out** to pay out money. □ *Come on, dub up!* □ *Just how much do you expect me to dub out this time?*

duchess a costermonger's wife. (A costermonger is a man who sells fruit and vegetables from a barrow, on the street; a barrowboy.) □ *You could tell she was a real duchess, covered from head to toe in pearlies.* □ *The costermonger and his duchess were very interesting people.*

duck a score of zero in some sports, especially cricket. □ *I'm afraid I scored a duck again.* □ *Well, a duck isn't the end of the world.*

duck and dive to hide. (Rhyming slang.) □ *It's too late to duck and dive, Boris. The police are here.* □ *He's ducking and diving to avoid his creditors.*

the **duck-pond** the Atlantic Ocean. □ *Oh, he's across the duck-pond just now, on business in New York.* □ *People think nothing of hopping over the duck-pond nowadays.*

ducks AND **ducky** darling, dear, etc. (A familiar form of address to or from a woman.) □ *Hello ducks, fancy some fun tonight?* □ *Fancy going down the pub, ducky?*

duck's disease short legs. □ *You may have just a touch of duck's disease my love, but to me they are lovely little legs nevertheless.* □ *You can tell which one is Harry. He's the one with duck's disease.*

ducky 1. cute; charming. □ *Isn't she ducky?* □ *What a ducky girl she is.* **2.** See ducks.

duck(y) bumps gooseflesh; goose pimples. (Jocular.) □ *It was so cold I was covered in ducky bumps in no time.* □ *I could feel duck bumps all over as I realised the full audaciousness of my idea!*

duff 1. counterfeit, broken, useless, or worthless. □ *I don't want any more of your duff radios.* □ *What a duff deal that turned out to be.* **2.** to fail to strike a golf ball. □ *Woops! I've duffed that shot.* □ *He's a terrible golfer, duffing just about every other swing he takes at a ball.*

Duke of Kent rent. (Rhyming slang.) □ *How much is your Duke of Kent?* □ *That money is for this month's Duke of Kent.*

Dunlop (tyre) a liar. (Rhyming slang.) □ *The fact is, he's just a Dunlop tyre.* □ *Anyone who told you that is a Dunlop.*

dunny 1. a cellar. (Scots usage.) □ *We keep aw sorts o' strange things doon oor dunny.* □ *The polis found him hiding in a dunny.* **2.** an underground passageway. (Scots usage.) □ *She widna go doon the dunny 'cos it was too dark.* □ *Dinny make me go back doon the dunny, Daddy! (Don't make me go back down that underground passageway, Father!)*

dustbin lid a child. (Rhyming slang, linked as follows: dustbin lid ≈ [kid] = child.) □ *Is this dustbin lid yours?* □ *She is a most irritating dustbin lid.*

dust-up a fight. □ *Mark got into a bit of a dust-up with Brian.* □ *There was a dust-up at the party that ruined the evening for everyone.*

dusty an old person. □ *He's a pleasant dusty.* □ *The dusty was waiting outside the office for him.*

dusty answer an unsatisfactory or brusquely negative reply. □ *He offered her a dusty answer and did not hang around for her reaction.* □ *I think you've just got your answer, and it's a dusty answer indeed.*

ear basher AND **ear-holer; ear-wigger 1.** a haranguer, nagger, or remonstrator. □ *You quite enjoy being an ear-holer, don't you?* □ *If you want to be an ear-wigger, please go and be one to someone else.* **2.** someone who is overly loquacious. □ *I wish that ear basher would just shut up for a change.* □ *Look, you ear-wigger, please be quiet and give my ears a rest!* **3.** an overhearer of a conversation; an eavesdropper. □ *I'd take care not to discuss anything important within range of that ear basher, if I were you.* □ *That ear-wigger seems to pick up every detail that matters.*

ear-holer See ear basher.

early bath a departure or termination which is unexpectedly early. (Originally a sporting metaphor.) □ *He was forced to take an early bath when they found out he was cooking his expenses.* □ *Arthur said he'd had enough and was taking an early bath.*

early days too soon for something to have yet happened. □ *Hold on, it's early days yet!* □ *I know it's early days, but I think we may be on to something here.*

earner a profit made by criminal activities. (Criminal cant.) □ *He got an earner out of that last burglary.* □ *To make an earner from stuff you steal, you've got to find a buyer.*

ear-wigger See ear basher.

ease to take time off or to relax. (Police slang.) □ *The policeman took five minutes to ease.* □ *Don't even think of easing when the sergeant is around.*

easy as you know how quite easy. □ *Oh, in the end it was easy as you know how.* □ *There's no problem. You'll find it easy as you know how.*

easy meat something that is easy to obtain. □ *That money was easy meat, wasn't it?* □ *If you're looking for easy meat, take a walk through these doors.*

easy-peasy very easy. (Childish.) □ *Simple! Easy-peasy, even!* □ *How do you manage to make everything look so easy-peasy?*

eau-de(-Cologne) the telephone. (Rhyming slang, linked as follows: eau-de(-Cologne) ≈ (tele)phone.) □ *My mobile eau-de-Cologne went off, and I had to leave the meeting.* □ *I'll have somebody call me during the meeting on me eau-de to get me out of it.*

ecilop the police. (Criminal's backslang.) □ *The ecilop are looking for you. What have you done?* □ *If the ecilop turn up, I'm not here, okay?*

eckies AND **exes** expenses incurred in the course of work. □ *He made a profit out of his eckies.* □ *I can't approve these exes.*

eefink a knife. (Backslang.) □ *I could tell from the way his cuff broke that there was a eefink strapped to his leg.* □ *Swiftly and silently his eefink found its way up under Rocko's ribs. All over a silly bit of skirt.*

eelacs scales. (Backslang.) □ *Where you put the eelacs to weigh this lady's fish, Sid?* □ *I think he's nobbled the eelacs.*

eenob a bone. (Backslang.) □ *He took a nasty knock on his eenob there, wot really hurts.* □ *Any eenobs for the dog?*

ekker exercise, particularly at university or school. □ *The truth was, he just loathed ekker.* □ *Every Thursday, the afternoon was given over to ekker of all sorts.*

elephant intoxicated due to drink. (Rhyming slang, linked as follows: elephant['s trunk] ≈ drunk.) □ *She was really elephant, and Molly had to take her home.* □ *Joe and Arthur kept on knocking them back till they were both elephant.*

elevenses a light refreshment or snack taken mid-morning. □ *Do you take elevenses here?* □ *We stop for elevenses every day, about ten-thirty.*

Elmer a (male) American tourist in Britain. □ *The Elmer says he's looking for the Loch Ness monster.* □ *Do you think we should tell the poor Elmer that he's unlikely to find Nessie in Putney Reservoir?*

enough to be going on with AND **something to be going on with** sufficient for the moment. □ *Seven courses and twenty bottles of wine will be enough to be going on with, I assure you.*

□ *Could we have something to be going on with, until the whole thing is ready?*

enough to make a cat laugh very funny. □ *Funny? It was enough to make a cat laugh!* □ *Harry's jokes can be funny enough to make a cat laugh at times.*

erdy a person without imagination; someone who is conventional and earthbound. (From the German *Erde*, meaning "earth" or "the Earth.") □ *What's a erdy like that doing around here?* □ *I'm sorry but we really don't need another erdy working here.*

Errol (Flynn) the chin. (Rhyming slang.) □ *He punched me right on the Errol Flynn.* □ *You can tell it's Harry 'cos he's the one with the huge Errol.*

esclop See slop.

exes See eckies.

exob a box. (Backslang.) □ *What's in the exob, guv?* □ *Mum, Sid's just come in with a great big exob.*

fab fabulous. □ *What a fab stereo that is!* □ *Your pad is not what I'd call fab. Just okay.*

face like the back (end) of a bus AND **face that would stop a clock; face like the side of a house** a spectacularly unattractive visage. (Normally used of the face of a woman or girl.) □ *Memorable? I'll say, she's got a face like the back end of a bus.* □ *You could say that when you looked into her eyes, time stood still, but then it is a face that would stop a clock.*

face like the side of a house See face like the back (end) of a bus.

face that would stop a clock See face like the back (end) of a bus.

faff a fuss. □ *Don't make such a faff! It's almost sorted.* □ *Why do you have to turn the simplest things into such a faff?*

faff about AND **faff around; flap around** to hesitate, dither, or fuss about. □ *Instead of faffing about, could you try working for a change?* □ *That's enough flapping around.*

faff around See faff about.

fair dos equitable shares. □ *Oh come on, fair dos! We all deserve the same.* □ *No, Jack gave us all fair dos I must say.*

a fair few AND **a good few** a large number. □ *There were a fair few folks at the church this morning.* □ *It'll take a good few payments like that to clear your debts.*

fair treat a very pleasurable experience. □ *Today was a fair treat. When can we do that again?* □ *The office party was a fair treat, I suppose.*

fall for it to become pregnant. □ *When I fell for it, I wondered what to do.* □ *I hear Sally has fallen for it.*

farmers haemorrhoids. (Rhyming slang, linked as follows: Farmer [Giles] ≈ [piles] = haemorrhoids.) □ *She's got to go into hospital* to get her farmers dealt with. □ When the wife's got the farmers she gets in a foul mood.

favourite excellent; ideal. □ This is a favourite day! □ Mary's got herself a favourite of a new job.

feather-bed someone to make someone very comfortable. □ Now, we're not going to feather-bed you, you know. □ I don't expect you to feather-bed me.

feel someone's collar to arrest someone. (Police.) □ The cops want to feel Harry's collar. □ Let's feel this hooligan's collar.

fiddle 1. to swindle, cheat, or lie. □ Bruno fiddled him out of his money. □ Don't try to fiddle me. I know the score. **2.** a difficult or frustrating task. □ The task I was given was a fiddle, for sure. □ This job is a real fiddle.

fiddler a swindler, cheater, or liar. □ That filthy fiddler told the police where I was. □ Harry is a certified fiddler. Don't trust him with a penny!

field of wheat a street. (Rhyming slang.) □ She stood on the field of wheat and cried. □ There he was, walking down the field of wheat.

fife and drum the buttocks. (Rhyming slang, linked as follows: fife and drum ≈ [bum] = buttocks.) □ She needs some jeans that will flatter her fife and drum. □ With a fife and drum like hers, it'll have to be flattened a lot before jeans will do any flattering.

the **filth** the police. □ Here comes the filth! □ The filth are out to get me, you know.

fine and dandy brandy. (Rhyming slang.) □ He handed me a glass of fine and dandy and we sat down. □ Any more of that fine and dandy, squire?

fingers 1. a pickpocket. □ The fingers tried a snatch, but the punter turned around at the wrong time. □ Watch out for fingers at the racetrack. **2.** a policeman. □ Think about how the fingers on the beat is affected by this cold. □ The fingers stopped at the door, tried the lock, and moved on.

finnip a five pound note. □ Burnside slipped him a finnip and faded into the fog. □ For a finnip, the tramp led Burnside to the place where the crate still lay in the alley.

fireman's hose a nose. (Rhyming slang.) □ *I want some glasses that sit in just the right place on my wonderful fireman's hose.* □ *What a fireman's hose on that guy!*

fish-eaters a knife and a fork. (Especially when used for eating a fish dish.) □ *It's not often we get the fish-eaters out around here.* □ *We are supposed to use fish-eaters for eating a fish, you know.*

fist 1. a hand. □ *If your fists so much as brush by my jacket again, you are finished!* □ *Get your fist off my car!* **2.** handwriting. □ *Well, I could read his fist—just about.* □ *Try to write in a reasonable fist if you can.*

fit someone up to frame an innocent person for a crime. (Police.) □ *The police here are always fitting people up.* □ *No, they're not. They only fit up people when they can't find genuine evidence.*

fit-up 1. a temporary stage. □ *He climbed onto the fit-up and declaimed the whole of Hamlet's soliloquy.* □ *We built the fit-up over there, but then we were told to move it.* **2.** the framing of an innocent person for a crime. (Police.) □ *It's a fit-up!* □ *No, it's not a fit-up, Otto. The evidence is overwhelming.*

fit-up company a travelling theatrical company. □ *I spent many years travelling around with a fit-up company.* □ *There are very few fit-up companies left. I blame television.*

fiver a five pound note. (Compare with **tenner**.) □ *This thing only cost me a fiver.* □ *Give him a fiver, and let's get away from here.*

fixture a planned sporting event. □ *The next big fixture is on Saturday.* □ *Are you planning to attend the fixture?*

flaff around to behave in a confused or agitated way. □ *Don't flaff around, tell me what's really wrong.* □ *If you flaff around like this we can't help.*

flanker a trick; a swindle; a deal that may not be quite honest. □ *What sort of flanker did you get ripped off with?* □ *Gerry has a new money-making flanker, but he hasn't made any yet.*

flap around See faff about.

flapjack a lady's powder compact. □ *I think I've left my flapjack in the ladies' room.* □ *She flipped open her flapjack and powdered her nose.*

flaps the ears. □ *He was grabbed by the flaps and forcibly removed from the premises.* □ *Pull back your flaps, this is worth hearing!*

flash of light a gaudily dressed person, particularly a woman. (Rhyming slang, linked as follows: flash of light ≈ [bright] = gaudy.) □ *I'm sorry but we really don't need another flash of light working here.* □ *What's a flash of light like that doing around here?*

flat spin 1. an almost horizontal spin by an aircraft. □ *Oh lord, he's gone into a flat spin!* □ *Fear not, he knows how to get out of a flat spin.* **2.** panic or excitement. □ *I was in a flat spin for a while, I'm afraid.* □ *Try not to get into a flat spin again, Arthur.*

flatters flat. □ *I say, your lawn is really flatters, eh?* □ *What a flatters tummy you have, Belinda.*

flavour of the month a sarcastic name for the current fashion. □ *So, are tartan ties flavour of the month?* □ *Why do you always have to wear the flavour of the month, then?*

flea-pit a rundown or dilapidated cinema. □ *If you think I'm going to sit and watch a film in a flea-pit like that, think again.* □ *Our local cinema really was a flea-pit by the time it closed down.*

Fleet Street the collective name for London's newspapers. (Fleet Street was the centre of London's printing business from about 1500 onwards. Newspapers' offices began moving out in the 1980s, and by the mid-1990s all had left. However, this is still their collective name.) □ *Let's see what Fleet Street makes of this in tomorrow's papers.* □ *I think the whole of Fleet Street is outside wanting to interview you, sir.*

flies' cemetery a cake consisting of a layer of currants sandwiched between shortbread layers. □ *I love flies' cemetery.* □ *Have another slice of my aunt's delicious flies' cemetery.*

flim any banknote which has a face value of five pounds sterling. □ *He put a number of flims into the top pocket of my shirt and said that there were plenty more to be had if I asked no questions.* □ *That'll be 15 please, sir. Or 10 in flims, if you prefer.*

flimsy 1. thin paper. □ *The fragile crockery was all wrapped up in flimsy.* □ *Where did you find all that flimsy?* **2.** a copy made on thin paper. □ *Make a flimsy of this and send it off to the head office.* □ *He opened a box which turned out to be full of some very interesting flimsies.* **3.** women's underwear made from very fine material. □ *She stood there in nothing but her flimsies.* □ *Oh, I don't think I could wear a flimsy like that!*

floater 1. a government stock certificate considered to be acceptable collateral for a loan. □ *Yes, the bank will accept floaters.* □ *What's the face value of your floater?* **2.** an error. □ *What a floater! You must be embarrassed.* □ *Well, that was a bad floater.* **3.** an uncommitted voter. □ *He won't say which party he supports. Put him down as a floater.* □ *There's an awful lot of floaters around here.* **4.** a drowned corpse. (Police, etc.) □ *There's a floater in the river.* □ *We've got to get the floater onto dry land first.* **5.** a sausage in soup. □ *Floaters are always acceptable to Otto.* □ *A serving of soup and floater came next.* **6.** a spot before the eyes. (Usually used in the plural.) □ *Harold's gone to see his doctor about these floaters he's been getting.* □ *Are floaters serious?*

flob to spit. (Childish.) □ *Angry? I could've flobbed!* □ *None of your flobbing in here!*

flowery (dell) a prison cell. (Rhyming slang.) □ *You won't find Jerry here. He's found himself back in the flowery dell.* □ *Another two years in the flowery. He felt utterly depressed.*

fly a kite 1. to propose a plan that is known to be doubtful. □ *I know it's not certain to work, but I think it's worth flying a kite.* □ *Why did you fly such a ridiculous kite, John?* **2.** to smuggle things in or out of prison. □ *My girl will fly a kite for me.* □ *They caught a warder trying to fly a kite.* **3.** to write a letter begging for money. □ *It's sad to see a man like that reduced to flying a kite like this.* □ *You'd be surprised how often you do get money when you fly a kite.*

fly-boy AND **fly man** a man who lives by his wits or cunning. □ *There are a lot of fly-boys around here, so watch out.* □ *How can anyone ever trust a fly man like him?*

fly man See fly-boy.

foodie someone obsessed about food. □ *Of course he's a foodie! Have you ever seen him not eating?* □ *The foodies all sit over there, near the kitchen.*

footer AND **footy** the game of football. (Soccer.) □ *Anyone for a game of footer?* □ *The lads are playing footy in the park.*

footling unimportant; trivial. □ *He came up with a stupid, footling suggestion. It was pathetic, really.* □ *It was just a footling little place.*

Footsie The Financial Times Stock Exchange Index. □ *How's the Footsie behaving?* □ *The Footsie's gone up nicely today.*

footy See footer.

for good and all AND **once (and) for all** finally; conclusively; in order to finally remove any doubt. □ *I'm gonna take care of you for good and all!* □ *I would like to get this ridiculous problem settled once for all.*

fork and knife a wife. (Rhyming slang.) □ *My fork and knife disapproved of the film.* □ *I've got to go home to my fork and knife.*

form 1. a criminal's prison or police record. □ *Does Otto have form?* □ *Form? You bet Otto has form.* **2.** a procedure. □ *There's a form for this sort of thing.* □ *All right, what's the form?* **3.** a situation. □ *What kind of form do you have there now?* □ *So how do we get ourselves out of this form we're in, eh?*

fourpenny one 1. a scolding. □ *Tom got a fourpenny one for his part in the prank.* □ *Her mother gave her a fourpenny one when she finally got home.* **2.** a push or shove. □ *I gave him a fourpenny one and he just fell over, honest!* □ *What was that fourpenny one for, eh?*

France and Spain rain. (Rhyming slang.) □ *Oh no, France and Spain again.* □ *Don't just stand out there in the France and Spain!*

frank and fearless a discussion. (From the cliché.) □ *Time for a frank and fearless, eh?* □ *OK, we'll have a frank and fearless now.*

fraught risky; dangerous. □ *Your plan is, let's say, fraught.* □ *You really are in a fraught situation here, you know.*

French loaf four pounds sterling. (This is an example of that rare beast, rhyming slang that depends upon backslang to make the connection. In the following, ruof—or rouf—is backslang for four. The rhyming slang linking is thus: French loaf ≈ [ruof] = four pounds sterling.) □ *A French loaf? For that?* □ *Burnside slipped him a French loaf and faded into the fog.*

fresher a freshman. □ *Bob's a fresher at the university now.* □ *There was a gaggle of fresher in the bar.*

frightener a scare. □ *Gosh, that was a right frightener, wasn't it?* □ *She does not like frighteners.*

frit frightened; terrified. □ *She's a very frit person. Try not to frighten her off.* □ *I feel a little frit every time I have to fly.*

frog and toad a road. (Rhyming slang.) □ *He was driving along the frog and toad when it happened.* □ *I hate travelling on that frog and toad.*

frog in the throat a boat. (Rhyming slang.) □ *We sailed away in his frog in the throat.* □ *Three men sat in their frog in the throat out there for hours, just fishing I think.*

frogspawn a sago or tapioca pudding. (Childish. Sago is a common children's "milk pudding" that is popular in Britain.) □ *Yuch! I hate frogspawn!* □ *Now, you eat up all your frogspawn. It's really yummy.*

from a child since infancy or childhood. □ *Oh, he's been like that from a child.* □ *From a child she brought me up.*

from here on in from this point forward. □ *From here on in we do it my way.* □ *I want everything clear from here on in.*

froth-blower a beer-drinker. □ *Harry's certainly a froth-blower.* □ *Oh, there's a lot of froth-blowers around here!*

fubsy a short and fat person. □ *Even a fubsy like that has to earn a living.* □ *What does the fubsy want?*

fug stale or smoky air. □ *There was a terrible fug in the room when we got there.* □ *We got rid of the fug by opening the widow.*

fuggy stale or airless. □ *It was so fuggy, I could hardly breath.* □ *This is far too fuggy for me.*

full belt AND **full bore; full tilt** maximum speed. □ *She passed me at full belt a few miles back. What's up?* □ *We were going along the motorway at full tilt when this cop car spotted us.*

full blast See full bottle.

full bore See full belt.

full bottle AND **full blast** as fast or as loud as possible. □ *As soon as he got onto the motorway, he put his foot down and was travelling at full bottle.* □ *The whistle blew full blast and woke everyone up.*

full marks 1. the highest possible examination score. □ *Congratulations! You scored full marks!* □ *If he got full marks, how could anyone fail?* 2. a recognition of excellence. □ *Well, I think you deserve full marks for that performance.* □ *Work like that really is worth full marks.*

full of beans lively; high spirited; energetic. □ *What a wonderful day! I feel so full of beans this morning!* □ *It's wonderful to see John so full of beans again after the difficult time he had.*

Full stop! AND **Period!** That is all!; Finally, without exception, extenuation, or extension. □ *Right, that's it, full stop!* □ *I'm not saying one more word, period!*

full tilt See full belt.

full whack the full price. □ *I had to pay the full whack.* □ *I never pay full whack—on principle!*

funk (out) to shrink or evade a duty, responsibility, or challenge. □ *No more funking will be tolerated around here.* □ *He funked out of that one, somehow.*

G

gaff 1. a cheap public amusement hall or theatre. □ *Don't you go near that gaff again, my lad!* □ *They are always having fights in that gaff. I don't know how it keeps its licence.* **2.** a building that is someone's home. □ *I stood outside his gaff and waited.* □ *Where's your gaff, son?* **3.** to cheat. □ *She gaffs every single customer that comes her way. She doesn't know any other way to operate.* □ *Don't try to gaff me. I wasn't born yesterday, you know.* **4.** a criminal venture. □ *The cops turned up right in the middle of the gaff.* □ *The whole gaff was a stupid idea in the first place anyway.*

gammy 1. injured. □ *Tom's gammy and needs some help.* □ *Fred had a little accident, and he's pretty gammy.* **2.** permanently lame. □ *He's sort of gammy since that football game.* □ *I've got a gammy leg, you know. I'll catch up with you later.*

gannet someone who gobbles down large quantities of food; a greedy person. (Crude. From the perceived propensity of the sea bird of this name to consume whole fish in such a manner.) □ *Get out of here, you gannet!* □ *Of course he's a gannet! Have you ever seen him not eating?*

gap site a plot of land between buildings that is considered large enough to accommodate another building. □ *We found a lovely little gap site in Southern Street.* □ *They're building a new house in that gap site.*

garn an expression of disbelief. (Derived from *go on*.) □ *Really? Garn!* □ *Garn, that's all crap.*

gash 1. pointless, broken, or useless. □ *What a gash deal that turned out to be.* □ *I don't want any more of your gash promises.* **2.** additional, extra, or not required. □ *There's a gash TV set in the bedroom, if you want to borrow it.* □ *Why have we got all these gash chairs in here?*

gasper a cigarette. □ *Got a gasper, pal?* □ *He got out the gaspers and passed them around.*

gasping desperate. □ *She was gasping for it.* □ *Oh him! He's always gasping for something or another.*

gates of Rome home. (Rhyming slang.) □ *It's not much but it's me gates of Rome.* □ *There, after all these years, I was in my gates of Rome once more.*

gauch out AND **gouch out** to pass out under the influence of drugs. □ *After taking the stuff, Gary gauched out.* □ *After the fix, Gert waited patiently to gouch out.*

gazump to raise a selling price, usually of a house or other property, after informally accepting an offer to buy at a lower price. □ *They tried to gazumph the price just before exchanging contracts.* □ *I just knew that that seller was going to gazump us!*

the gents' a men's toilet. (An abbreviation of *gentlemens'*.) □ *Is there a gents' somewhere close?* □ *Joe has gone to the gents'.*

George Raft a draught. (Rhyming slang.) □ *There's a terrible George Raft blowing from that window.* □ *He caught a chill from a George Raft and is in bed.*

get AND **git** a foolish person. □ *Please don't call me a get. I do my best.* □ *Who's the git in the bright orange trousers?*

get a grip on one's knickers to take control of oneself. □ *Look, it's not the end. Get a grip on your knickers!* □ *So I got a grip on my knickers and it was all right after that.*

get a packet See cop a packet.

Get knotted! AND **Get lost!** Go away!; Leave me! □ *Get knotted, you're bothering me!* □ *Quit following me. Get lost!*

Get lost! See Get knotted!

get no change to get no help. □ *You'll get no change from that quarter.* □ *I got no change there.*

get (one) out of one's pram to cause one to become very excited or angry. □ *Well, that news really got him out of his pram!* □ *Now, don't get out of your pram when you hear my news.*

get one's books AND **get one's cards 1.** to be fired from a job. □ *Why did I get my books?* □ *I want you to make sure this character gets his cards right now.* **2.** to get oneself fired from a job. □ *Simon got his books when he told his boss what he really thought.*

□ *Getting your cards from that great job was really, really stupid, you oaf!*

get one's cards See get one's books.

get oneself spliced to get oneself married. □ *I hear you got yourself spliced, Paul.* □ *When did you two get yourselves spliced, then?*

get one's head down 1. to lie down to rest or to go to sleep. □ *He's got his head down through there.* □ *I'm just going to get my head down for half an hour.* **2.** to concentrate upon the task in front of one. □ *I'm very busy and must get my head down.* □ *If you get your head down, you can soon be finished.*

get one's knickers in a twist 1. to become angry. □ *I'm trying not to get my knickers in a twist, but it's hard.* □ *Now, don't get your knickers in a twist. Relax.* **2.** to become confused. □ *Please try to avoid getting your knickers in a twist once more.* □ *I'm sorry but I've got my knickers in a twist again, I think.* **3.** to become excited and upset. □ *Don't get your knickers in a twist. It's going to be all right.* □ *She really had her knickers in a twist, I tell you.*

get one's monkey up to become very angry. □ *Now you're getting his monkey up.* □ *Don't get his monkey up.*

get something cracked to solve a problem or difficulty; to learn a skill. □ *I've got it cracked!* □ *After I get it cracked, the rest'll be easy.*

get stroppy to become angry. □ *Oh, Willy is always getting stroppy about something.* □ *Willy can get stroppy when he talks about the accident.*

get the bullet See get the sack.

get the chop See get the sack.

get the push 1. to be sent away. □ *Sent to Australia? You mean, I'm getting the push?* □ *What did I do to get the push like this?* **2.** See get the sack.

get the road See get the sack.

get the sack AND **get the bullet; get the chop; get the push; get the road; get the wallop** to be dismissed from one's employment. □ *Poor Tom got the sack today. He's always late.* □ *I was afraid that Sally was going to get the wallop.*

get the staggers to lose one's ability or talent. (Sports.) □ *Well, I don't think he's going to be running in the Olympics after getting* *the staggers like he has.* □ *Oh no, I've got the staggers. I'm finished now.*

get the wallop See get the sack.

get up someone's nose to greatly irritate someone. □ *So I made a mistake! I wish you'd stop getting up my nose about it.* □ *Getting up his nose is not going to correct the mistake.*

get weaving 1. to get started. □ *Let's get weaving on this.* □ *The sooner we get weaving, the sooner we'll get there.* **2.** to move along quickly. □ *We better get weaving now.* □ *We can still do it if we get weaving.*

the **giddy limit** someone or something that is at, or just beyond, the acceptable. □ *That's it! That's just beyond the giddy limit!* □ *Whee! She's the giddy limit!*

giggle 1. a group of schoolgirls. □ *He looked up and saw a giggle of girls walking across the park.* □ *That giggle should all be at school just now.* **2.** a trivial but amusing person or thing. □ *Well yes, she is just something of a giggle I suppose.* □ *Even giggles have to earn a living—probably by being amusing if that's possible.* **3.** See giggle and titter.

giggle (and titter) beer. (Rhyming slang, linked as follows: giggle (and titter) ≈ [bitter] = beer.) □ *Have another pint of giggle and titter, Charlie.* □ *Hey, that's good giggle you've got here!*

ginger (beer) a ship's engineer. (Rhyming slang.) □ *This is Scotty. He's our ginger beer.* □ *The ginger told the captain it would be about two hours before the ship could be ready to sail.*

ginormous vast or huge. □ *A ginormous aircraft flew low over the village.* □ *Why are lawyers' fees always so ginormous?*

git See get.

give away (the) change to let slip confidential information. □ *Woops! I think I just gave away the change!* □ *Don't give away change tonight if you value your skin.*

give over to desist or cease. □ *Oh give over. I've had enough.* □ *If you don't give over I'll call the police.*

give someone a bell AND **give someone a shout** to telephone someone. □ *You'd better give her a bell to find out what's up.* □ *Harry asked for you to give him a shout.*

give someone a shout See give someone a bell.

give someone the benefit of one's thoughts See give someone the side of one's tongue.

give someone the chop See give someone the sack.

give someone the pip to annoy someone greatly. □ *That remark gave her the pip, once she realised what it meant.* □ *The whole business began to give her the pip after a while.*

give someone the sack AND **give someone the chop** to dismiss someone from employment. □ *They had to give Paul the sack because he was so unproductive.* □ *I was afraid they would give me the chop.*

give someone the side of one's tongue AND **give someone the benefit of one's thoughts** to harangue, nag, or remonstrate. □ *I'll certainly give her the side of my tongue if she shows her face in here again!* □ *I'm here to give you the benefit of my thoughts, so shut up and listen!*

give something a bash AND **give something a go; give something a tumble** to attempt to achieve something. □ *Well, I'm prepared to give it a bash!* □ *Yes, I'd like to give the thing a tumble.*

give something a go See give something a bash.

give something a miss to stop doing or to fail to do something. □ *I'm going to give drinking a miss from now on.* □ *It would be a good idea for all of you to give smoking a miss, too.*

give something a tumble See give something a bash.

glam glamorous. □ *Some glam blonde sang a couple of songs, and then the band played again.* □ *He has a real glam place nowadays.*

Glasgow boat a coat. (Rhyming slang.) □ *That's a ridiculous Glasgow boat. I won't wear it.* □ *Anyone seen me Glasgow boat?*

the glooms a fit of depression. (Irish usage.) □ *The glooms? If you don't get yourself sorted out in short order, I'll give you the glooms all right!* □ *I think it would be smart to leave him alone just now. He's got the glooms.*

go a bundle on someone to think highly of someone. (Always in the negative.) □ *I'm afraid I did not go a bundle on Susan. No, not at all.* □ *Apparently Susan didn't go a bundle on you either, since you didn't ask.*

go (a)round the houses to avoid or to delay coming to the point. □ *Instead of going around the houses yet again, could we finally* *come to the point, please?* □ *Why did you go round the houses instead of just coming right out and asking?*

gob 1. the mouth. □ *Shut your gob and get on with your work.* □ *Have I ever told you that you have an ugly gob?* **2.** a slimy lump. □ *I can't eat these gobs of so-called food.* □ *There was a gob of the stuff on the plate, but I wasn't going to eat it.*

gobslutch a person with disgusting or filthy personal habits. (Crude.) □ *You gobslutch, that's just disgusting!* □ *If you're going to be a gobslutch, you can be one somewhere else.*

gobsmacked AND **gobstruck** flabbergasted; entirely astonished or dumbstruck. □ *Clearly, he was gobsmacked by the news.* □ *What she said really gobstruck me.*

gobstruck See gobsmacked.

go down 1. to leave university without a degree. □ *If I don't pass these degree exams I'll have to go down.* □ *Roger went down after five years at the college.* **2.** to be accepted. □ *We'll just have to wait for a while to see how all this goes down.* □ *The proposal didn't go down very well with the manager.* **3.** to be arrested. (Underworld.) □ *Lefty didn't want to go down for a job he didn't do.* □ *Mr Big said that somebody had to go down for it, and he didn't care who.* **4.** to be sent to prison. □ *He'll go down for ten years.* □ *"You're going down for sure," said the judge.*

go down a treat AND **go down well** [for something, especially food or drink] to be greatly enjoyed. □ *That looks as if it would go down a treat.* □ *It really went down well.*

go down well See go down a treat.

the **God rep** a chaplain or padre. □ *The God rep's a good guy.* □ *He had to go and see the God rep about something or other.*

the **gods 1.** the highest gallery level of a theatre. □ *Sitting in the gods is an experience you have to have at least once.* □ *The cheapest seats are in the gods, of course.* **2.** the people sitting on the highest gallery level of a theatre. □ *He prefers to sit among the gods, as they are—he says—a nicer bunch.* □ *There were few gods in the top balcony that evening.*

go for a burton 1. to be killed, particularly in battle. □ *A large number of our best went for a burton taking that hill, and for what?* □ *If we try to take that hill like we did the last one, a lot more of us will go for a burton for sure.* **2.** to become broken or destroyed. □ *I'm afraid the thing's gone for a burton.* □ *If you drop it, it will assuredly go for a burton.*

goggle box a television set. □ *A huge goggle box sat there, dominating the room.* □ *She flicked off the goggle box as we entered.*

gold watch whisky. (Rhyming slang, linked as follows: gold watch ≈ [Scotch] = whisky.) □ *A wee drop of the gold watch is always acceptable round here.* □ *He said thank you with a bottle of gold watch, since you ask.*

golf widow a wife left alone while her husband plays golf. (Compare with bridge widow.) □ *There's a lot of us golf widows around here, especially at weekends.* □ *Why don't you come along to the next meeting of Golf Widows Anonymous?*

go like the clappers 1. to travel very rapidly. □ *Go like the clappers! We're very late!* □ *If we're to get there on time we must go like the clappers.* **2.** to work very hard. □ *If you go like the clappers you should be finished on time.* □ *We must go like the clappers. There is no time to lose!*

good few See fair few.

good form the proper way to behave. □ *We are looking for good form around here, you understand.* □ *What's the good form on this situation?*

Good for you! See Good on you!

Good on you! AND **Good for you!; Good show!** Well done!; Congratulations! □ *Good on you! That's just what we want!* □ *Good show! I'm glad you won.*

Good show! See Good on you!

good wicket 1. a cricket game that's going well. □ *We've got a good wicket today.* □ *A good wicket makes all the difference.* **2.** a good situation to be in. □ *Well, that's a good wicket to be in!* □ *I'm looking for a good wicket.*

go off the boil to lose the initiative; to lose interest. □ *I think he's gone off the boil for that plan.* □ *If you don't keep up interest the public will go off the boil.*

googly a ball bowled so that it spins in the opposite way to that expected. (Cricket.) □ *Take care, he does a deadly googly.* □ *I can't cope with googlies.*

googly-merchant a bowler of googlies. (Cricket.) □ *This bowler is a real googly-merchant.* □ *If he's a googly-merchant, I'm a goner.*

goose and duck a lorry. (Rhyming slang, linked as follows: goose and duck ≈ [truck] = lorry.) □ *There are too many geese and ducks using this small residential road.* □ *Why is there a huge goose and duck parked outside our house?*

goosegog a gooseberry. □ *Goosegogs make you . . . well, you know.* □ *My wife makes goosegog jam every year.*

goose('s neck) a cheque. (Rhyming slang.) □ *All right, I'll take your goose.* □ *I'm afraid my goose's neck'll bounce.*

gorblimey See blimey.

gorilla one thousand pounds sterling. (Compare with monkey and pony.) □ *Who the blazes is going to be daft enough to give you a gorilla for that?* □ *This car is worth at least twenty gorillas.*

gormless foolish or witless; none too smart. □ *You gormless fool, you've wrecked it!* □ *Then this gormless idiot comes up and asks her for a dance.*

go round the haystack to visit the toilet. (Rhyming slang, linked as follows: go round the haystack ≈ [back] = toilet.) □ *Just a moment while I go round the haystack.* □ *Gotta go round the haystack!*

go short of something to do without something. □ *I'm afraid we'll just have to go short of food until we get back to base, Captain.* □ *I don't see why we should have to go short of anything.*

go something to use something. □ *I could go a cup of tea.* □ *This company could go a serious injection of cash.*

go spare 1. to become extremely angry or upset. □ *Now don't go spare! It's not as terrible as it looks.* □ *Are you surprised she went spare when she saw it?* **2.** to become surplus or no longer required. □ *These ones in the corner are going spare.* □ *If you have any that go spare, we'll take them.* **3.** to go to waste. □ *It's a shame that all that food had to go spare.* □ *There's four hundred quid going spare here you know.*

goss gossip. (Teens.) □ *Enough of this goss—on with the show!* □ *I like to listen in on other people's goss.*

go to earth to hide. (As an animal does in its burrow.) □ *He's gone to earth to avoid his creditors.* □ *It's too late to go to earth, Boris. The police are here.*

go to the loo to urinate. (Crude.) □ *Well, going to the loo does relieve the pressure of all that beer!* □ *I'm just going to the loo.*

got something off pat to have learned something perfectly. □ *As soon as I got the wording off pat, they changed the words.* □ *The secret of effective speechmaking is not to get the exact words off pat, but to get the meaning off pat in your mind so that when you stand up you know what message you want to impart. The words will come easily then.*

gouch out See gauch out.

governor AND **guv; guv'nor 1.** one's employer. (Also a term of address.) □ *My governor told me to move these boxes.* □ *What do you want done next, guv?* **2.** one's father. □ *My governor told me to get a job.* □ *I'll ask my guv'nor if I can go.*

gozz a gossip session, especially on the telephone. □ *Is this gozz going to go on all night?* □ *If you must have gozzes like that, get your own phone.*

grab a pew AND **take a pew** to take a seat; to sit down. □ *Come in, Fred. Just grab a pew anywhere you see a chair. This place is a mess.* □ *Just take a pew, and we'll have our little talk.*

graft 1. hard work or effort. □ *It's called graft. Try it sometime.* □ *These young ones don't know what hard graft really means.* **2.** shady dealings or corruption, especially bribery. □ *The amount of graft going on in here is beyond belief.* □ *How can we stop this epidemic of graft?*

grafter 1. a hard worker. □ *You won't be sorry, he's a real grafter.* □ *I only want grafters working on this.* **2.** a criminal. □ *Greg has become such a grafter that no one speaks to him any more.* □ *There's nothing but grafters in that pub.*

gran a grandmother. □ *The kids love visiting their gran.* □ *I love my gran.*

grand one thousand pounds sterling. □ *That car probably cost about twenty grand.* □ *Four grand for that thing?*

grasshopper a policeman. (Rhyming slang, linked as follows: grasshopper ≈ [copper] = policeman.) □ *The grasshopper stopped at* *the door, tried the lock, and moved on. □ Think about how the grasshopper on the beat is affected by this cold.*

the Great Smoke See Big Smoke.

green fingers the wonderful ability to garden and grow pot plants. □ *Helen has green fingers and can work wonders with plants.* □ *If I had green fingers, I could grow my own roses.*

Gregory (Peck) 1. a bank cheque. (Rhyming slang.) □ *"Don't worry," he smiled, "a Gregory Peck will be just fine."* □ *I made my Gregory out and handed it to him.* **2.** the neck. (Rhyming slang.) □ *Have you noticed? Harry's got a really thick Gregory Peck.* □ *Look, you are a real pain in the Gregory. OK?*

grice to watch trains, as a hobby or pastime. □ *There are a lot of people gricing on that bridge most Saturdays.* □ *What's the fascination in gricing?*

gricer an enthusiastic watcher of trains. □ *There they are. The gricers are out in force today.* □ *Why does anyone want to be a gricer?*

grizzle 1. the fretful cry of a young child. □ *The child's grizzle has been there in the background all night now.* □ *How can anyone ignore grizzle for so long?* **2.** to whine or complain. □ *Some people grizzle because they don't have anything else to do.* □ *Come on, don't grizzle all the time!*

grotty 1. ugly, dirty, or disgusting. □ *If you must be grotty, go and do so somewhere else, thank you.* □ *That's really grotty, don't go in there.* **2.** grotesque; highly undesirable. □ *Let's not see another grotty movie tonight.* □ *What is this grotty stuff they serve here?* □ *It's not grotty!*

ground bones powdered milk. □ *I keep some ground bones in there in case we run out of the liquid kind.* □ *Oh, I prefer ground bones actually.*

grue fear; terror. □ *Just thinking of that gives me the grue every time.* □ *She gets the grue whenever she has to give a talk.*

grumbly a clumsy or dull person. □ *Even a grumbly like that has to earn a living.* □ *What does the grumbly want?*

grungy dirty; smelly; unwashed. □ *A strange, grungy smell hung over the whole area.* □ *The trouble is that the grungy little tyke usually has good information.*

gubbins 1. a fool. □ *You gubbins! You've buttered the tablecloth!* □ *Those gubbins are at it again. Spend, spend, spend.* **2.** machinery. □ *But what's all this gubbins for, Martin?* □ *Get this gubbins working. That's what you're paid for!* **3.** rubbish. □ *You've certainly got a lot of gubbins here.* □ *What are we supposed to do with this gubbins?*

guest beer a beer from one brewery on sale in a public house owned by another. □ *How about a guest beer before you go, Charlie?* □ *Give my friend here a guest beer.*

Gunga Din and squatter's daughter gin and water. (Rhyming slang.) □ *He gave me a Gunga Din and squatter's daughter and left me alone.* □ *Like another Gunga Din and squatter's daughter, mate?*

gunge any messy or sticky substance. □ *What sort of gunge is that?* □ *We opened the jar and found it was full of some disgusting gunge.*

gunge something up to clog up with gunge. □ *Who gunged up the sink again?* □ *Gunging up one long-range oil pipeline with impurities can cost millions of pounds to repair.*

gungy messy; sticky; spoiled; ruined or worn out; nasty. □ *Get your gungy feet off the sofa.* □ *All that gungy stuff is blocking the drain.*

gurk to belch. □ *Try not to gurk at table, Johnny.* □ *She gurked quietly behind her hanky, so no one would notice.*

guv See governor.

guv'nor See governor.

had a basinful had enough; had as much as one can stand. □ *I've had a basinful. I'm off.* □ *That's it, I've had a basinful.*

hail and rain a train. (Rhyming slang.) □ *There are hail and rains passing here all the time.* □ *Take the hail and rain—that's the easy way to get there from here.*

half half a pint. (Usually beer, when ordered in a pub.) □ *Just make mine a half, thanks.* □ *Come on, you must have more than just a half!*

half (a) bar AND **half a nicker** half of one pound sterling. □ *Lend us a half bar for the fruit machine, mate.* □ *Come on, even you can afford this. It's only half a nicker!*

half a dollar twelve and a half pence (formerly two shillings and sixpence, or half a crown). (This dates from the 19th century, when there were four U.S. dollars to the pound for many years. A crown is a former British coin with a face value of one quarter of a pound.) □ *For half a dollar, what have you got to lose?* □ *What does half a dollar buy you nowadays?*

half a mo half a moment. □ *Half a mo, what did you say?* □ *I'll be there in half a mo.*

half a nicker See half (a) bar.

half a ton fifty pounds sterling. □ *Can you lend me half a ton till pay-day?* □ *All right, here's half a ton. Don't spend it all in one shop.*

half-inch to steal. (Rhyming slang, linked as follows: half-inch ≈ [pinch] = steal.) □ *Everyone half-inches nowadays, it seems.* □ *It may seem harmless to half-inch from your employer, but it's still theft.*

hamps See hampsteads.

hampsteads AND **hamps** the teeth. (Rhyming slang, linked as follows: Hampstead [Heath] ≈ teeth.) □ *That horse has a nice set of hampsteads.* □ *I may be on me last legs, but me hamps are still all me own.*

handbag someone [for a woman] to attack or hit someone. □ *Mrs Thatcher had a reputation for handbagging her opponents.* □ *If you come any closer, young man, I'll handbag you!*

handsome excellent; very satisfactory. □ *This wine is really handsome!* □ *Boy, what a handsome fishing rod this is.*

happy chappie one who is delighted with one's situation. (Always used in the negative, or ironic.) □ *I don't think he's a happy chappie, doctor.* □ *What a collection of happy chappies you are I must say!*

happy clappy a member of certain kinds of evangelical churches, where congregations regularly participate in services with frequent bursts of applause, which can appear meaningless to the casual observer. □ *There was a convention of happy clappies in our town last week.* □ *What does a happy clappy actually do—apart from clap, that is?*

harbour all right. (Rhyming slang, linked as follows: harbour [light] ≈ (all) right.) □ *Don't worry, it's all harbour again now.* □ *It's fine—it's all harbour.*

hard cheese AND **hard lines** hard luck. □ *Now that's really hard cheese.* □ *We have had our share of hard lines.*

hard done by mistreated or ill served. □ *I'm hard done by!* □ *You don't know the meaning of hard done by.*

hard lines See hard cheese.

hard neck See brass neck.

harpic crazy; demented. (From the advertising for Harpic, a household cleaning agent, that claimed it would "clean round the bend.") □ *I'm not really as harpic as I seem.* □ *I'm not harpic. I just can't make it work.*

hassle someone See chivvy someone.

have a slate loose to be somewhat mentally unstable. □ *This child's has a slate loose, I think.* □ *I feel like I must have a slate loose.*

have it away to escape from prison. □ *You'll never have it away from this place.* □ *Oh yeh? I'll have it away. You'll see.*

have one's chips 1. to be unable to avoid punishment; to be unable to avoid losing a struggle. □ *It's no use, I've had my chips.* □ *He'll have had his chips with me when I catch him!* **2.** to have died. □ *Just for a moment I was afraid I'd had my chips, but the moment passed.* □ *The parrot had had it's chips by the time I got home.*

have one's collar felt to be arrested. □ *If you want to have your collar felt, just keep on behaving like that.* □ *Harry's just had his collar felt.*

have someone for breakfast to defeat someone with ease. □ *Careful, she'll have you for breakfast.* □ *I'm afraid they had our team for breakfast again.*

have someone on to trick or delude someone. □ *You're having me on!* □ *Come on, we'll have her on.*

have someone's guts for garters to take extreme retribution against someone. (Normally uttered in the form of a threat.) □ *If you try anything like that again, I'll have your guts for garters.* □ *I told him I'd have his guts for garters.*

have someone up to bring someone to justice. □ *They'd have Mr Big up if they could just find the evidence.* □ *Why are they having up that poor guy? It's not his fault.*

hearth rug a dupe; a fool. (Rhyming slang, linked as follows: hearth rug ≈ [mug] = dupe/fool.) □ *That old hearth rug came past again, muttering something incoherent under his breath.* □ *Sometimes I'm such a hearth rug. I really messed the whole business up, didn't I?*

heavens above love. (Rhyming slang.) □ *Just look at the two of them. It's heavens above!* □ *It was obvious they were in heavens above.*

helmet a uniformed police officer. □ *We need some helmets down here urgently.* □ *I was never more pleased to see a helmet.*

her indoors a wife or girlfriend. □ *Her indoors is looking for you.* □ *I'll ask her indoors if we can come over this weekend.*

hide up to protect or shield someone wanted by the police. □ *I've got to hide up. The fuzz are after me.* □ *You can't hide up in here, son!*

hide-up a hiding place. □ *Where do you think his hide-up is?* □ *I think Otto's gone into his hide-up.*

hiding to nothing a situation that can only lead to failure. □ *Let's face it, we're on a hiding to nothing here.* □ *I don't intend to let this become a hiding to nothing, thank you!*

high jump 1. any severe punishment. (Compare with in for the high jump.) □ *It's the high jump for you, my lad!* □ *What else but the high jump do you expect after what you've done?* **2.** the **high jump** dismissal from a job; the sack. □ *The high jump is what I am afraid of.* □ *The boss gave them all the high jump.* **3.** AND **long jump** an execution, particularly a hanging. □ *The high jump was carried out at dawn this morning.* □ *There's to be another long jump next week.*

hit someone or something for six 1. [with *something*] to score six runs by hitting a cricket ball over the boundary of the playing field without the ball touching the ground after it leaves the bat. □ *Wonderful! He hit it for six!* □ *Hit the ball for six again!* **2.** [with *something*] to demolish an argument. □ *Your argument is easy to hit for six.* □ *Come on, that theory was hit for six ages ago.* **3.** [with *someone*] to successfully subject someone to a sudden shock or attack. □ *We really were hit for six by the news.* □ *If he does that again I'll hit him for six all right.*

hive something off to separate something from a larger entity. □ *I hear they plan to hive off the pharmaceuticals division from the rest of the company.* □ *Why would I want to hive off that bit? It's the most profitable.*

hols holidays. □ *I'm going to America for the hols.* □ *What are you doing for your hols this year, Charles?*

Holy Ghost 1. the post. (Rhyming slang.) □ *The postman handed her her Holy Ghost.* □ *Anything in the Holy Ghost for me today?* **2.** the winning post. (Rhyming slang.) □ *Me horse was first past the Holy Ghost and that's all that matters, innit?* □ *He stood at the Holy Ghost and watched the horses rushing past.* **3.** toasted bread. (Rhyming slang.) □ *Any more of that Holy Ghost?* □ *I'm going to make myself some Holy Ghost. Fancy some?*

holy nail AND **Royal Mail** court bail. (Rhyming slang.) □ *Any chance of holy nail, guv?* □ *If he gets Royal Mail again, I'll eat my hat.*

home and dry safe after taking a risk. □ *I don't feel home and dry here.* □ *Don't worry, you're home and dry now.*

homework a girlfriend; a wife. □ *I wish I had as lovely homework as her to go back to every evening!* □ *I think I'm in love with Harry's new homework.*

honk 1. a drinking spree; a wild party. □ *Jed's last honk lasted nearly a week.* □ *The guys went off on the honk to end all honks.* **2.** to empty one's stomach; to vomit. (Crude. Scots usage. Onomatopoetic.) □ *I can hear someone in the cludge honking something awful. (I can hear someone in the toilet being violently sick.)* □ *Who honked on the driveway?* **3.** a bad smell; a stink. □ *Where is that terrible honk coming from?* □ *I just can't stand that honk.* **4.** to emit a bad smell; to stink. □ *If you've got to honk like a badger's backside, do so a long way from me.* □ *When we opened the room it honked very badly.*

Honkers Hong Kong. □ *Meet Simon, just back from Honkers.* □ *I'm off to Honkers on business next week.*

hooked AND **hooky** stolen. □ *I know they must have hooked my handbag after I left it on the table, officer.* □ *I think these computer memory chips are hooky.*

hooky See hooked.

Hoover something (up) to devour rapidly or greedily. □ *The children really Hoovered up the food put out for them.* □ *If you Hoover your food like that again, Johnny, Mummy will be angry.*

Hop it! Go away!; Get lost! □ *Get out of there! Hop it!* □ *Why don't you just hop it?*

hop off (one's twig) 1. to leave very suddenly. □ *Well, I must hop off my twig now.* □ *Time for us to hop off now, I think.* **2.** AND **drop off the twig** to die. □ *He dropped off the twig when his plane crashed during a training flight.* □ *For a minute, I thought I was going to hop off my twig.*

horrorscope a horoscope. □ *We all look at the horrorscope in the paper every morning when we have our coffee.* □ *Do you believe your horrorscope?*

horse and cart an anal release of intestinal gas; a noise or smell associated with this. (Crude. Rhyming slang.) □ *Oh lord! Who made that horse and cart?* □ *The pungent scent of a recent horse and cart hung in the air.*

horses for courses capabilities and requirements that are well matched together. □ *You'll be fine. Remember—horses for courses.* □ *Let's try to find horses for courses, people.*

hot bills newly issued treasury bills. □ *The bank bought a lot of these hot bills.* □ *The government sometimes has trouble shifting hot bills.*

hottie(-tottie) a hot-water bottle. □ *Aunt Mary set off to bed with her hottie-tottie as usual.* □ *I'd prefer a hottie to an electric blanket.*

hotting joyriding in a stolen car. □ *The kids killed in the crash had been hotting.* □ *There's a lot of hotting going on in this area.*

the **House of Lords** a men's toilet. (Crude. A euphemism.) □ *Can you tell me where I'll find the House of Lords?* □ *I need to use the House of Lords urgently!*

house to let a bet. (Rhyming slang.) □ *I'm placing a house to let on that horse.* □ *Did you win your house to let?*

hum 1. a bad smell. □ *There is a terrible hum in here.* □ *Let's see if we can get rid of this hum.* **2.** to emit a bad smell; to stink. □ *The fact is, the tramp was humming badly.* □ *The food, which had been left to rot, hummed in a most offensive manner.*

hundreds and thousands tiny coloured sweets sometimes sprinkled over food items, such as cakes, in order to decorate them. □ *Johnny likes it when his mum puts hundreds and thousands all over a cake.* □ *She spilt the hundreds and thousands, which then got into everything.*

hung on someone emotionally dependent upon someone. □ *Look, she's become quite hung on you so you're going to have to be careful.* □ *It's important that your patients don't become hung on you.*

I

ice cream a man. (Rhyming slang, linked as follows: ice cream [freezer] ≈ [geezer] = man.) □ *What does the ice cream want?* □ *He's a rather surprising ice cream.*

idiot box AND **idiot's lantern; box** a television set. □ *You spend too much time watching the idiot box.* □ *What's on the box tonight?*

idiot's lantern See idiot box.

if the cap fits if it appears to be true. □ *If the cap fits, so be it.* □ *Well, maybe. But only if the cap fits very well indeed.*

I'll be there a chair. (Rhyming slang.) □ *Sit on that I'll be there and say not a word!* □ *He produced the strangest I'll be there from a cupboard.*

I'm afloat a coat. (Rhyming slang.) □ *I've lost my I'm afloat.* □ *That's a ridiculous I'm afloat. I won't wear it.*

I'm so whisky. (Rhyming slang, linked as follows: I'm so [frisky] ≈ whisky.) □ *Get out the I'm so, and let's have a drink.* □ *The bottle was empty. More I'm so, I think!*

I'm willing five pence. (Rhyming slang, linked as follows: I'm willing ≈ [shilling] = five pence. Five pence in modern currency is equivalent to one shilling in pre-1971 currency units.) □ *An I'm willing? For what?* □ *That'll be an I'm willing, missus.*

in a maxe confused or bewildered. □ *Leave her be. She's completely in a maxe this afternoon.* □ *Don't tell me you're in a maxe yet again!*

in and out a nose. (Rhyming slang, linked as follows: in and out ≈ [snout] = nose.) □ *He threatened to punch me right on the in and out!* □ *How did you get an in and out like that?*

in for a penny, in for a pound 1. once started, there's no way out. □ *Well, in for a penny, in for a pound. We've no choice.* □ *If we must do it, let's do it. In for a penny, in for a pound!* **2.** all or

86

nothing. □ *In for a penny, in for a pound! We must succeed now!* □ *Once we pass that point it's in for a penny, in for a pound.*

in for the high jump AND **in for the long jump 1.** facing very severe problems or punishment. □ *I'm in for the high jump—I just know it!* □ *If they catch you, you're certainly in for the long jump.* **2.** due to be hanged; liable to be hanged. □ *There in the courtroom, for the first time, he really appreciated that he could be in for the high jump.* □ *They don't mess around in that country. Drug smugglers are in for the long jump.*

in for the long jump See in for the high jump.

in narrow circumstances impoverished. □ *No, I can't lend you money. I'm in narrow circumstances myself.* □ *Since the factory closed, everyone in this town is in narrow circumstances.*

Innit? Isn't it? (Eye-dialect, used in the examples in this dictionary.) □ *It's okay if I take one of these, mum, innit?* □ *Innit cold today!*

in-off to pocket one ball by bouncing it off another. (Billiards and snooker.) □ *He did a brilliant in-off to pocket the black ball.* □ *I looked at the table and realised I was going to have to play the in-off of my life if I was to have any chance of winning the championship.*

in pop in pawn. □ *Get it out of pop or go and buy a new one.* □ *My watch is already in pop.*

in Queer Street in serious trouble, especially financial. □ *His business went bust and now he's in Queer Street.* □ *Not everyone in Queer Street is there by their own fault.*

insects (and ants) trousers, knickers, or pants. (Rhyming slang.) □ *You're not properly dressed without insects and ants.* □ *She opened the drawer, removed all the insects there, and left the room with them.*

instant mum a foster mother. □ *She was brought up by an instant mum.* □ *Henrietta is an instant mum.*

in the cart in a losing, embarrassing, or difficult situation or predicament. □ *Really, we're lucky not to be in the cart in a far worse way than we are.* □ *Let's be honest: we're in the cart.*

in the country anywhere upon a cricket field that is a long way from the wickets. □ *Yes, I think we could say that's in the country.* □ *Try to hit more of the balls out in the country.*

in the noddle See in the noodie.

in the noodie AND **in the noddle; in the nuddie** naked. □ *All these nudists were running about playing volleyball or something in the noddle.* □ *It's the thought of barbecues in the nuddie that would put me off.*

in the nuddie See in the noodie.

in the (pudding) club pregnant. □ *Then this woman, very obviously in the pudding club, started to complain, too.* □ *I can see she's in the club.*

in two ticks very soon. □ *Hold on, I'll be there in two ticks.* □ *We'll be done in just two ticks!*

Irish a wig. (Rhyming slang, linked as follows: Irish [jig] ≈ wig.) □ *I wear just a little Irish to cover up a shiny spot.* □ *Is that guy wearing an Irish, or does his scalp really slide from side to side?*

jack 1. a policeman or detective. □ *See that jack over there? He lifted me once.* □ *The jacks will catch up with you some day.* **2.** an odd-job man. □ *Ask the jack if he needs any help.* □ *Why do we need this jack?*

jack all AND **naff all** nothing. □ *We've got jack all for you here. Shove off.* □ *Nice words, but worth naff all.*

Jack and Jill 1. a hill. (Rhyming slang.) □ *There's a castle on that Jack and Jill.* □ *Let's climb the Jack and Jill and look at the castle.* **2.** a pill. (Rhyming slang.) □ *Come on, mum, you know you've got to take your Jack and Jill.* □ *Get mum her Jacks and Jills please, love.*

Jack Horner a corner. (Rhyming slang.) □ *There was a nice-looking chair in the Jack Horner.* □ *As the car came round the Jack Horner it rolled over twice.*

jack-in-office a self-important, minor civil servant. □ *Oh, he's just another jack-in-office. He's not important.* □ *If you must be a jack-in-office, could you please at least be an efficient one?*

jack someone or something in AND **pack someone or something in 1.** to ruin or destroy someone or something. □ *I think he's trying to jack us in.* □ *Why should anyone jack this great venture in?* **2.** to abandon someone or something. □ *Oh, I jacked that idea in some time ago.* □ *We have had to pack in our expansion plans, I'm afraid.*

Jack Straw a worthless man. □ *I like the look of this Jack Straw.* □ *The Jack Straw was not there.*

Jack the Ripper a kipper. (Rhyming slang. A kipper is a herring which has been cured by smoking.) □ *He likes a Jack the Ripper for breakfast.* □ *I could never see the attraction of Jack the Rippers.*

the jakes a men's toilet, especially a public one. (Crude.) □ *Where's the jakes?* □ *The jakes is around the corner.*

jam-jar a tram-car. (Rhyming slang.) □ *There used to be jam-jars in every major British city but now there are very few.* □ *They've built a new jam-jar system in Manchester.*

jammy 1. easy. □ *I did not think that opening a bank vault could be so jammy.* □ *What a jammy little job that was!* **2.** lucky. □ *Why, you jammy sod!* □ *You were really, really jammy that time!* **3.** profitable. □ *This is a jammy little business you have here.* □ *If you must work, make it jammy, I always say.*

jam roll parole. (Rhyming slang.) □ *He smiled. It was jam roll time, at last!* □ *Now this lot are really well behaved, 'cause they're all hoping for jam roll.*

jam sandwich a police car. (Many are white with a conspicuous horizontal red band along each side.) □ *The jam sandwich drove forward, blocking my exit.* □ *Watch it! That's a jam sandwich!*

jangle to chat or gossip. □ *My, isn't Mary jangling a lot today?* □ *He's always jangling on about something or other, but I like him.*

jank cheek; impudence. □ *What jank! Who does she think she is?* □ *Any more jank like that and he'll get everything he deserves.*

J. Arthur (Rank) a bank. (Rhyming slang. The kind of bank where money is kept. J. Arthur Rank was a British filmmaker.) □ *That's the J. Arthur where I keep my money.* □ *When does yer J. Arthur Rank open today, then?*

Jeremiah a fire. (Rhyming slang.) □ *I told him to put more coal on the Jeremiah.* □ *There was a big Jeremiah near here last night.*

jerks See physical jerks.

jiggle and jog a French person. (Offensive. Rhyming slang, linked as follows: jiggle and jog ≈ [Frog] = French.) □ *Why can you never be polite to jiggles and jogs?* □ *Y'know, Otto, if you call a French person a jiggle and jog, he's likely to get nasty.*

jiggy a jigsaw puzzle. □ *This jiggy is a real tough one.* □ *Can you help me with this jiggy?*

jill 1. a girl. (Probably from the nursery rhyme "Jack and Jill.") □ *What a beautiful jill she is.* □ *Hands off her! She's my jill!* **2.** a policewoman. □ *He still found it difficult to take jills, especially pretty ones, seriously.* □ *Otto could not believe that this tiny little jill had actually arrested him.*

jimmy 1. one pound sterling. (Rhyming slang, linked as follows: Jimmy [Goblin] ≈ [sovereign] = one pound sterling. A sovereign is a former coin with a face value equal to one pound.) □ *There's a thousand jimmies in this for you. But do it now!* □ *I could use a jimmy if you can spare one, guv.* **2.** to obtain entry to a place of public entertainment such as a sports stadium, cinema, etc., by trickery or deceit. □ *We jimmied our way into the stadium and saw the game.* □ *How did you ever jimmy your way in there?* **3.** See jimmy riddle.

Jimmy Prescott a waistcoat. (Rhyming slang.) □ *He had the strangest garishly coloured Jimmy Prescott you've ever seen in your life.* □ *Are Jimmy Prescotts not kinda dated nowadays?*

jimmy (riddle) an act of urination. (Crude. Rhyming slang, linked as follows: jimmy (riddle) ≈ [piddle] = urination.) □ *He went out to take a jimmy riddle.* □ *I've just got to go for a jimmy.*

Jim(my) Skinner AND **Lilley and Skinner** dinner. (Rhyming slang. Lilley and Skinner is a well-known store in London. Nobody knows who Jimmy Skinner was.) □ *Hey, where's me Jimmy Skinner?* □ *Right love, where are we going for our Lilley and Skinner tonight?*

jobsworth an official or employee who insists on strict adherence to petty rules. (From the phrase, "It's more than my job's worth . . .") □ *Oh, forget him. He's a real jobsworth if ever I saw one.* □ *I hate these petty jobsworth types.*

Joe Bloggs AND **Joe Soap** the average British man. □ *You may go for that choice, but do you really imagine Joe Bloggs would?* □ *Just because I'm only a Joe Soap doesn't mean I don't have an opinion, you know.*

Joe Soap See Joe Bloggs.

joey 1. an illegal package or parcel sent in or out of prison. □ *Is that a joey you've got there, Otto?* □ *How can he get a joey out to me?* **2.** a dupe, weakling, or fool. □ *Why do you have to be such a joey?* □ *That poor joey thinks he can convince them.*

Jo(h)anna a piano. (Rhyming slang.) □ *There she was, playing the old Johanna.* □ *There used to be a Joanna in that corner.*

john(darm) a policeman. (From the French *gendarme*, meaning "policeman.") □ *The johndarm stopped at the door, tried the lock,* *and moved on.* □ *Think about how the john on the beat is affected by this cold.*

John Hop a policeman. (Rhyming slang, linked as follows: John Hop ≈ [cop] = policeman.) □ *The John Hops are here looking for you again, Joe.* □ *What have you been doing to interest that John Hop this time?*

Johnny Rutter butter. (Rhyming slang.) □ *Half a pound of Johnny Rutter, please.* □ *I like Johnny Rutter on me bread. Don't you?*

jokey funny, in the sense of "unusual" rather than "comical." □ *What a jokey sort of place this is.* □ *I better warn you, Otto's a bit jokey right now.*

jolly D. See jolly dee.

jolly decent See jolly dee.

jolly dee AND **jolly decent; jolly D.** considerate; helpful. □ *Thanks, that's jolly dee of you.* □ *You know, you're being jolly decent about this.*

josser a foolish person. □ *Then this josser comes up and asks her for a dance.* □ *You right josser! You've buttered the tablecloth!*

jubbly money. □ *How much jubbly do you need, then?* □ *Sorry, I can't afford it, I've no jubbly.* □ *Lovely jubbly!*

the **jug (and pail)** jail. (Rhyming slang.) □ *Take it easy. I don't want to end up in the jug.* □ *A couple of days in the jug and pail would do you the power of good.*

jug handles AND **jug-lugs** protruding ears. (Usually in the plural.) □ *Pull back your jug handles, this is worth hearing!* □ *He was grabbed by the jug-lugs and forcibly removed from the premises.*

jug-lugs See jug handles.

jumble miscellaneous used or discarded articles. □ *There's a big pile of jumble over there in that corner.* □ *Why do you never throw out this jumble?*

jumble sale AND **jumbly** a special one-day sale where articles of jumble are for sale. □ *The jumble sale raised a lot of money for the church.* □ *If the club needs funds, let's have a jumbly.*

jumbly See jumble sale.

jumper a ticket inspector on a train or bus. □ *We all had to produce our tickets when the jumper appeared.* □ *The jumper is asking for your ticket, Charlie.*

jump the queue See queue jump.

just a tick just a moment. □ *Just a tick. Can we have a word?* □ *Hold on! Just a tick!*

just the job AND **just the ticket** the perfect thing. □ *A nice cup of tea will be just the job.* □ *This little thing is just the ticket.*

just the ticket See just the job.

K

kahsi See carsey.

kangaroo petrol the supposed fuel of a car driven in a particularly jerky or jumpy manner. □ *Look at this. He seems to have got some of that kangaroo petrol in his car.* □ *You'd think he always bought kangaroo petrol, from the way he drives.*

Kate and Sidney steak and kidney pie. (Rhyming slang.) □ *Oh good. Kate and Sidney is always my favourite!* □ *Fancy some more Kate and Sidney?*

kay-rop poches pork chops. (Backslang.) □ *Fancy some kay-rop poches, dead cheap?* □ Q: *Where've you got them kay-rop poches from?* A: *Don't ask.*

keep to reside, particularly at Cambridge University. □ *I was most unhappy when I started keeping at Cambridge.* □ *Do you intend to keep at the College?*

Keep shtoom! Keep quiet! □ *Be quiet. Keep shtoom!* □ *Keep shtoom! Don't let them know we're here!*

Keep your pecker up. 1. Remain cheerful. □ *Keep your pecker up, it's not all that bad!* □ *Don't ruin everyone's fun, keep your pecker up!* **2.** Don't give up hope. □ *Keep your pecker up, it's going to turn out all right.* □ *Don't lose hope, keep your pecker up.* **3.** Don't lose courage. □ *Keep your pecker up, we're going to beat them!* □ *Be brave, keep your pecker up.*

Kermit a French person. (Rhyming slang, linked as follows: Kermit [the Frog] ≈ [frog] = French. Offensive.) □ *I'm sorry but we really don't need another Kermit working here.* □ *What's a Kermit like that doing around here?*

kettle a steam-powered locomotive. □ *We spend our weekends restoring old kettles.* □ *That kettle certainly produced lots of steam, smoke, noise . . . and everything.*

key to own or drive a car. (Derived from the driver being the person who has its key.) □ *Yeh, he keys that car.* □ *Get out your car and key it over to Charlie's.*

kharsie See carsey.

khazi See carsey.

kiddywinks an affectionate name for children. □ *So, how are all the kiddywinks today?* □ *Well, kiddywinks, what shall we do next?*

King Dicky a bricklayer. (Rhyming slang, linked as follows: King Dicky ≈ [brickie] = bricklayer.) □ *There's a King Dicky here to see you.* □ *We need more King Dickys if we're to get this thing built on time.*

kip 1. to sleep. □ *He's upstairs kipping. Can he phone you back later?* □ *He'll kip for about another hour.* **2.** a bed. □ *Well, it's time I was getting into the old kip.* □ *Get out of that kip and get up and get going!*

kip down to go to sleep. □ *I'm just going to kip down for half an hour.* □ *He's kipped down through there.*

kipper 1. an affectionate name for a small child. □ *It's all right, kipper, it's all right.* □ *What's wrong now, kipper?* **2.** a torpedo. □ *How many kippers does this submarine carry, Captain?* □ *They launched a kipper at the target, but missed.* **3.** a particularly wide necktie. □ *The attacker was wearing a bright kipper, officer.* □ *Pardon me sir, is this your kipper?*

kipper and bloater a car. (Rhyming slang, linked as follows: kipper and bloater ≈ [motor] = motorcar.) □ *Good lord, what sort of kipper and bloater do you call that?* □ *I don't think much of your kipper and bloater!*

kissing tackle the mouth. □ *Shut your kissing tackle!* □ *Put this in your kissing tackle and chew it up.*

klondyke 1. to obtain money with ease. □ *Come on, we're gonna klondyke here!* □ *He's always looking to klondyke.* **2.** to catch herring in the North Sea, salt and barrel them at sea, and sail directly to Russia (previously Germany) to sell them. (From the huge profits made.) □ *He makes a lot of money klondyking.* □ *They klondyke because they make a great deal of profit.*

klondyker the owner or captain of a ship that klondykes. □ *They say these klondykers can make a fortune.* □ *Ask that klondyker if it's true.*

knacker to exhaust. □ *If he tries to do that all day he'll soon knacker himself.* □ *I'll knacker myself if I keep that up!*

knackered exhausted. □ *Poor Ted really looks knackered.* □ *I feel too knackered to go to work today.*

knees-up a lively gathering or party. □ *I haven't had a knees-up like that in years.* □ *That was some knees-up at Tom's the other night.*

knicker bandit a small-time thief who steals from clothes-lines. □ *Well, seems like we've got a knicker bandit at work in this area.* □ *It turned out the knicker bandit was not exactly a pervert. He was selling what he stole at a car boot sale!*

Knickers! a term of disgust or contempt. □ *"Knickers!" he said, and walked away, ignoring their cries.* □ *Knickers! There's no way I'm going to do that.*

know one's age to act in accord with one's age or maturity. (Often used in the negative.) □ *Why does he do this? He doesn't seem to know his age.* □ *Know your age! You're not a child any more.*

konk See conk.

L

Lady Godiva five pounds sterling; a five pound note. (Rhyming slang, linked as follows: Lady Godiva ≈ [fiver] = five pounds sterling.) □ *Have you got a few Lady Godiva you can spare?* □ *These things cost more than just a few Lady Godivas, you know.*

Lady Muck a self-important and pretentious woman. (Compare with **Lord Muck**.) □ *Oh, these two really do think they're Lord and Lady Muck.* □ *I cannot stand that Lady Muck.*

lakes crazy. (Rhyming slang, linked as follows: Lakes [o' Killarney] ≈ [barmy] = crazy.) □ *I'm not lakes. I just can't make it work.* □ *I'm beginning to feel more lakes the longer I stay around here.*

lallies legs. (Always in the plural.) □ *Look at the lallies on that bird!* □ *Is she the one with the lovely lallies?*

lamp 1. to strike; to hit. □ *Harry lamped him one right on the jaw.* □ *I got a heavy lamping from Harry yesterday.* **2.** to look at someone or something. (The lamps are the eyes.) □ *I lamped the paper and then threw it away.* □ *Here, lamp this tyre for a minute. It's low isn't it?* **3.** to throw. □ *When I said you should get rid of it, I did not mean you should literally lamp it out the window.* □ *She was lamping all her old clothes away.*

lance-jack a lance-corporal. (Military.) □ *He's been made up to lance-jack.* □ *What does the lance-jack want?*

Land of Hope soap. (Rhyming slang, from the patriotic song "Land of Hope and Glory.") □ *A bar of Land of Hope, please.* □ *What have you done with the Land of Hope, woman?*

land someone one to hit someone. □ *Harry's livid and out to land you one for what you did.* □ *He landed me one as I walked over to my car.*

laugh and joke a smoke. (Rhyming slang.) □ *He stopped for a minute for a laugh and joke.* □ *He had a laugh and joke and then went back to work.*

laughing gear the mouth. □ *Why don't you just close your laughing gear for a moment and listen.* □ *How do we get her laughing gear closed so the rest can talk?*

laugh like a drain to laugh loudly. □ *Funny? I laughed like a drain.* □ *The woman laughs like a drain at the least provocation.*

lay-down a sleep. □ *I could use a lay-down before I have to get to work.* □ *I need a lay-down before I get started again.*

leave (something) over to leave something for action or consideration later. □ *Leave it over. I'll take a look later.* □ *Oh leave over Charlie. I don't have time for this just yet.*

left and right a fight. (Rhyming slang.) □ *Well, if that's really how you feel, let's have a left and right!* □ *The left and right was a bit of a failure as the other side failed to show!*

legless very intoxicated due to drink or drugs. □ *They were both legless. They could only lie there and snore.* □ *Tipsy? Legless, more like!*

lemon squash a wash. (Rhyming slang.) □ *Well, I'm off for a lemon squash now.* □ *He certainly needed to have a lemon squash.*

let-out an excuse; an alibi. □ *That's not a good reason. That's just a let-out.* □ *This is just a silly let-out.*

Let's be having it! Give it to me! □ *What have you done with it? Let's be having it!* □ *Let's be having it. We'll soon find it, you know!*

level peg with someone or something to perform equally well with someone or something. □ *Our software was level pegging with the others in the lab tests, but was much more expensive.* □ *Maria level pegged with the rest of the class in most subjects.*

ligger a sponger. □ *Get out of here you ligger, and earn your keep.* □ *I do not like or trust that ligger.*

light an eye. (Usually plural.) □ *Do you want me to poke your lights out?* □ *Open your lights and look out for the street names.*

light and dark a park. (Rhyming slang.) □ *After lunch, we went for a stroll in the light and dark.* □ *I like being able to look out over the light and dark from my flat.*

light blue **1.** a present or former student of Cambridge University. □ *He is a light blue, studying physics.* □ *I was not a light blue. I went to Oxford.* **2.** a present or former pupil of Eton College. □

An awful lot of prime ministers have been light blues. □ *Why are Eton College pupils called light blues?*

light of love the official in charge—the governor—of a prison. (Prisoners' slang. Rhyming slang, linked as follows: light of love ≈ [guv] = governor.) □ *The light of love here is a right sod.* □ *I was there four years and never saw the light of love yet.*

lig off someone to sponge. □ *You're not going to lig off me. Get yourself a job.* □ *He's been ligging off us for months.*

like billy-o with great vitality or speed. □ *I've been trying like billy-o to fix this machine all weekend.* □ *We were late and driving like billy-o when the accident happened.*

lilac effeminate. (Crude.) □ *A lilac man does not have to be gay, you know!* □ *He may have been lilac, but he gave us an amazing torrent of abuse.*

Lilley and Skinner See Jim(my) Skinner.

linen draper a newspaper. (Rhyming slang.) □ *This linen draper's only good for putting in the bottom of birdcages!* □ *I'm tired of reading this linen draper day after day. Can't we get a different paper?*

line of country a field or area of knowledge or expertise. □ *Computers are my line of country, I suppose.* □ *What's your line of country, then?*

Lionel Blair a chair. (Rhyming slang. From the name of a popular entertainer.) □ *He produced the strangest Lionel Blair from a cupboard.* □ *Sit on that Lionel Blair and say not a word!*

little Audrey the bull's-eye of a dart board. □ *His first dart was right on little Audrey. Amazing!* □ *Some people never manage to hit little Audrey.*

load of cods(wallop) AND **load of old cobblers; load of crap; load of guff** utter nonsense. □ *Don't give me that load of codswallop! I won't buy it.* □ *That's just a lot of load of guff.*

load of crap See load of cods(wallop).

load of guff See load of cods(wallop).

load of old cobblers See load of cods(wallop).

loaf the head; the brain. (Rhyming slang, linked as follows: loaf [of bread] ≈ head.) □ *That's using your loaf!* □ *Put your hat on your loaf, and let's go.*

local a neighbourhood pub. □ *You'll usually find our local is well attended in the evenings.* □ *The local is where you go to pick up all the gossip.*

lollipop 1. the police. (Rhyming slang, linked as follows: lollipop ≈ [cop] = policeman.) □ *See that lollipop over there? He lifted me once.* □ *The lollipop will catch up with you some day.* **2.** to inform the police. (Rhyming slang, linked as follows: lollipop ≈ [shop] = inform.) □ *Are you going to lollipop on me?* □ *I don't lollipop on no one.*

lollipop lady AND **lollipop man; lollipop woman** a school crossing patrol person. (From the shape of the sign that this person holds up to halt traffic.) □ *The school is looking for a new lollipop man or woman.* □ *The lollipop woman outside the local school really looks after the children well.*

lollipop man See lollipop lady.

lollipop woman See lollipop lady.

lollop to lounge about. □ *Don't lollop like that, Johnny.* □ *I don't like to see people lolloping instead of sitting correctly.*

lolly 1. money. □ *Sorry, I can't afford it, I've no lolly.* □ *How much lolly do you need, then?* **2.** sweets. □ *Mummy, can I have a lolly?* □ *I love lollies. I always have, ever since I was little.* **3.** a lollipop. □ *Remember Kojak? He always used to be sucking on a lolly.* □ *Come on, let's both get lollies to suck on.*

London fog a dog. (Rhyming slang.) □ *The London fog frightened the child.* □ *Why do you keep a London fog like that?*

long-eared stupid. □ *I'm very sorry, but the truth is that Otto is a long-eared oaf.* □ *Don't worry Otto, I don't think you're all that long-eared.*

long jump See high jump.

long lie time spent lying in bed longer than usual. □ *On Saturday morning I usually have a long lie.* □ *He's a lazy individual, always taking long lies.*

long pockets and short arms a psychological inability to spend money. □ *You'll be lucky! He's a severe case of long pockets and short arms.* □ *People with long pockets and short arms are also called "mean."*

longstop 1. the area of a cricket field behind the wicket keeper. □ *I'd like you to field in the longstops this afternoon, please.* □ *Who's that fielding at longstop?* **2.** a final chance or opportunity. □ *It's only a longstop, but worth a try.* □ *All right, here's a longstop for you.*

long-tongued long-winded; loquacious. □ *What a boring, long-tongued explanation that was.* □ *Could we have a less long-tongued story the next time?*

loo a toilet. (Possibly from the French *l'eau,* meaning "water.") □ *Where's the loo?* □ *The loo? Oh, it's along that passageway.*

look sharpish AND **look slippy** to get a move on. □ *Look sharpish! We're late!* □ *Come on, all of you! Look slippy!*

look slippy See look sharpish.

loop-the-loop soup. (Rhyming slang.) □ *There's nothing better than some loop-the-loop on a cold day.* □ *Fancy a bowl of loop-the-loop?*

Lord Muck a self-important and pretentious man. (Compare with Lady Muck.) □ *They've behaved like Lord and Lady Muck as long as we've known them.* □ *Lord Muck over there seems to think he can just summon you to his presence.*

love AND **luv; luvvy** a casual term of endearment to a stranger, particularly to or from a woman. □ *Are you all right, love?* □ *Right luvvy, you can't stay here.*

lucky budgie a lucky person. (Often ironic. Also a term of address.) □ *For once, I really felt I'd been a lucky budgie.* □ *Here was one lucky budgie, he thought.* □ *Some lucky budgie will have to clean up this mess.*

Lucy Locket a pocket. (Rhyming slang.) □ *Have you any change in your Lucy Locket?* □ *Get yer hand out of yer Lucy Locket, son.*

lumber someone or something with someone or something to encumber someone or something with someone or something inconvenient or unwanted. □ *It would seem they have lumbered us with this problem, like it or not.* □ *Don't try to lumber me with that character again ever!*

lump 1. an automobile engine. □ *He's spent hours out there trying to figure out what's wrong with the lump.* □ *There's something wrong. The lump won't turn over.* **2.** a stupid clod of a man.

☐ *I am not a lump! I am just sedate and pensive.* ☐ *Who is that lump leaning over the bar?* **3.** the **lump** the informal employment and payment of casual construction workers, without benefit of income tax and other such deductions. ☐ *People working the lump think they're getting one over the tax people, but I'm not so sure.* ☐ *The lump is much less common than it used to be.*

the **Lumpy Gravy** AND **Plain and Gravy; Pudding and Gravy; Soup and Gravy** the Royal Navy. (Rhyming slang.) ☐ *The Lumpy Gravy are always looking for the right kind of people.* ☐ *Paul's joined the Soup and Gravy.*

luv See love.

luvvy See love.

Maggie the one pound coin. (Given this name when introduced in 1983 during the premiership of Margaret Thatcher, on the grounds that it (and she) was "hard, rough at the edges and pretending to be a sovereign." The sovereign was a former British gold coin with a face value of one pound.) □ *It's three Maggies for that, mate.* □ *Will you take a Maggie?*

maggoty very intoxicated due to drink. (Irish usage.) □ *They were both so maggoty all they could do was lie there and snore.* □ *Joe and Arthur kept on knocking them back till they were both maggoty.*

make a bad fist of something to perform something badly. □ *I'm afraid I've make a bad fist of this.* □ *Don't make a bad fist of this one, too.*

make a bog of something to make a mess or muddle of something. □ *Well, we've really made a bog of things this time.* □ *Why did we let Otto make a bog of everything?*

make a good fist (of something) to do a good job. □ *This time, I must make a good fist of things.* □ *If you can make a good fist, you'll get rewarded.*

make a muck of something AND **make a poor fist of something** to bungle or to do a poor job of something. □ *I hope I don't make a muck of things this time.* □ *I really made a poor fist of this before.*

make a mull of something to perform badly. □ *Please try not to make a mull of this as you seem to have of everything else.* □ *Why do I always make a mull of these things?*

make a poor fist of something See make a muck of something.

make the running to take charge; to establish the pace. □ *Are you making the running here?* □ *We need someone to make the running.*

Malta dog a picturesque name for diarrhoea or a similar affliction, especially when suffered by visitors to Malta. □ *I had a little touch of the Malta dog the second day, but other than that we had a wonderful time.* □ *Most people blame the Malta dog on the water.*

man and wife a knife. (Rhyming slang.) □ *Bring your man and wife over here and cut this loose.* □ *What are you carrying a man and wife for?*

manor 1. the territory that an individual police station is responsible for. □ *The newly appointed Station Superintendent went out to look over his new manor.* □ *The manor needed proper policing and was about to get it.* **2.** one's local area, which one knows and where one is known. □ *Yes, I think we can say this village is my manor. I've lived here all my days.* □ *It's good to come home to one's manor after travelling around the world.*

marg margarine. □ *They say marg is better than butter, but I much prefer butter.* □ *Marg helps keep you fit.*

mark someone's card 1. to warn someone off. (From the action of a soccer referee who records a breach of rules in the card which each professional player must carry.) □ *I'm marking your card. Don't come back.* □ *He marked my card, but I don't really know why.* **2.** to tell someone what they want to know. □ *All right, I'll mark your card. Buy shares in Acme Company.* □ *I tried to mark his card as he wanted, but I don't think he got the point.*

Mary Blane a train. (Rhyming slang.) □ *Get the Mary Blane—that's the easy way to get there from here.* □ *There are Mary Blanes passing here all the time.*

marzipan a material that is used as bodywork filler on cars to remove—or rather, hide—the effects of accidents or corrosion. □ *Well, I'd say you've bought yourself some very expensive marzipan here.* □ *Marzipan—the cowboy car bodyworker's friend.*

mash mashed potatoes. □ *I like mash with my bangers.* □ *Pass me the mash, mum.*

masses lots; plenty. □ *When I have spaghetti, I just love masses of noodles.* □ *My uncle has just masses and masses of money.*

massy massive, solid, or bulky. □ *A truly massy man stood in the lobby.* □ *I don't want to live in such a massy house as this.*

mauley 1. a fist; a hand. □ *Get your mauley off my car!* □ *If your mauleys so much as brush by my jacket again, you are finished!*

2. handwriting; a signature. □ *Try to write in a reasonable mauley if you can.* □ *Well, I could read his mauley—just about.*

max someone to confuse someone. □ *Well, you've maxed me.* □ *I suspect you've maxed yourself into the bargain.*

measure one's length to fall flat upon the ground or floor by accident. □ *It was just a gentle tap, but still he measured his length.* □ *If you measure your length like that, something is wrong.*

me old cock a term of friendly address to a male acquaintance. □ *Come on, me old cock! I'll buy you a pint.* □ *I told me old cock here not to worry. It'll be all right in the end.*

mercy blow-through AND **mercy bucket(s)** thank you very much. (From the French *merci beaucoup*, which means this. An example of hobson-jobson.) □ *Mercy buckets! That was great!* □ *If she had just said so much as "mercy blow-through" it would have been nice.*

mercy bucket(s) See mercy blow-through.

the **merries** fairground rides. □ *Harry always likes going on the merries.* □ *I see there are some new merries this year.*

the **merry dancers** the aurora borealis, or northern lights. □ *Have you ever seen the merry dancers?* □ *The merry dancers can be spectacular, especially from northern Scotland.*

the **Met 1.** the Metropolitan Police, London's police force. □ *The Met are after me!* □ *Get away, get away! The Met are outside!* **2.** the Meteorological Office, which issues the official weather forecasts daily. □ *What does the Met say the weather is going to be?* □ *Met forecasts are usually quite good.*

Mick(e)y Mouse™ 1. a house, particularly a small one. (Rhyming slang. Probably from the world-famous mouse character by the same name, owned by The Walt Disney Company.) □ *This is a silly little Mickey Mouse.* □ *This mickey mouse may be small, but it's all mine.* **2.** to have a conversation with yourself. □ *Look at him—I think he's Mickey Mousing!* □ *Don't micky mouse! People will think you're crazy!*

Middle for diddle! a call to choose who is first to play in a game of darts by throwing one dart as close as possible to the centre of a board. □ *Right, let's play now. Middle for diddle?* □ *Middle for diddle! You throw first!*

mike 1. a period spent not working. □ *Oh, him? He's having some mike.* □ *Mike's on the mike again.* **2.** to avoid work. □ *Mike goes to great lengths to mike, of course.* □ *Mike your work just once more and you're out. Is that clear?* **3.** to hang about hopefully. □ *Oh, he's just miking.* □ *Don't waste your time miking. Nothing ever happens here.*

mild and bitter a mixture of mild beer and bitter beer. □ *Can I have mild and bitter, please?* □ *I do like this mild and bitter they have in here.*

milk-jug a dupe. (Rhyming slang, linked as follows: milk-jug ≈ [mug] = dupe.) □ *I think we've found the milk-jug we need, boss.* □ *I'm not sure you'll be glad you chose Otto for milk-jug when he eventually finds out.*

mill an automobile engine. □ *There's something wrong. The mill won't turn over.* □ *He's spent hours out there trying to figure out what's wrong with the mill.*

mince pie an eye. (Rhyming slang.) □ *He looked me right in the mince pie and assured me again that he was telling the truth.* □ *I think there's something wrong with me mince pies.*

The **mind boggles!** This is amazing!; This is unbelievable! □ *Oh boy! The mind boggles!* □ *The mind boggles! I don't know how that's possible!*

minder 1. a bodyguard, particularly of a criminal. □ *Mr Big is tiny, but his minder is huge.* □ *I don't think you want to meet his minder.* **2.** a pickpocket's assistant, who keeps the victim occupied and unaware. □ *Look how they operate! I'm sure that guy's the minder.* □ *The police caught the minder, but the dip got away.*

miss off AND **miss out** to avoid or omit. □ *I should be on the guest list. How did I come to be missed off?* □ *We'll miss out that stop as we are so short of time.*

miss out See miss off.

mittens 1. boxing gloves. □ *He pulled on his mittens and climbed into the ring.* □ *He held up his mittens for the umpire to inspect them.* **2.** handcuffs. □ *He slipped the mittens onto the arrested thief.* □ *The policeman clipped a spare set of mittens on his belt.*

mizzle to decamp or abscond. □ *Now don't you try to mizzle again, Sammy.* □ *The dog mizzled for a while but came back on her own accord.*

M'lud a barrister's term of respectful address to the judge when addressing him or her in open court; an abbreviation of *My Lord*. □ *M'lud, I believe my learned colleague may be in error on this point.* □ *I should like to bring the following evidence to the court's attention, M'lud.*

moaning minnie someone who is continually lamenting or complaining. □ *Sometimes I think you actually enjoy being a moaning minnie!* □ *You really are a terrible moaning minnie, you know.*

mob-handed in a group. □ *If we go in there mob-handed, it should not be a problem.* □ *They turned up mob-handed, and I was not going to argue.*

mock a trial or rehearsal of an examination. □ *How did you get on in your mock?* □ *The mocks are next week, you know.*

mocker a jinx. □ *All that character can utter is a string of mockers, it seems.* □ *Now there was a charming mocker!*

mod cons the facilities expected in modern property. (Estate agents' jargon. An abbreviation of *modern conveniences*.) □ *House for sale with all mod cons.* □ *We're only interested in houses that have all the usual mod cons and things.*

mog See moggie.

mogger See moggie.

moggie AND **mogger; mog** a cat. □ *Is this your moggie here? What's he called?* □ *Get that mog out of the refrigerator!*

Molly Malone a telephone. (Rhyming slang.) □ *The Molly Malone's been very busy all day today.* □ *The Molly Malone was ringing off the hook when I came in.*

money for jam AND **money for old rope** a profit for little or no effort or cost. □ *This is so easy, it's money for jam.* □ *Why is this so much money for old rope? What are we missing?*

money for old rope See money for jam.

mongy stupid. □ *Mike is so mongy when he's been drinking.* □ *What a mongy idiot I was!*

monkey five hundred pounds sterling. (Compare with **gorilla** and **pony**.) □ *He put a monkey into the top pocket of my shirt and said that there were plenty more to be had if I asked no questions.* □ *Who the blazes is going to be daft enough to give you a monkey for that?*

moody 1. fake, pretended, or counterfeit. □ *Sorry, it's a moody one.* □ *Otto's taken to selling moody jewellery.* **2.** a period or outburst of bad temper. □ *Don't work yourself up into a moody.* □ *You only have to look at them to see that they've been having a terrible moody.* **3.** meaningless or nonsensical talk; lies. □ *Boy, he can certainly churn out moody by the hour!* □ *That's just so much moody. Ignore it.*

mooey [of fruit or vegetables] rotten or overripe. □ *Get rid of these vegetables. They're mooey!* □ *No mooey stuff here thank you.*

moosh 1. to crush or squeeze. □ *I sat on my biscuits and mooshed them up into crumbs.* □ *He mooshed up the note and threw it upon the fire.* **2.** to kiss. □ *Let's go somewhere quiet and moosh.* □ *There are some teenagers in the back room, mooshing and so on.*

mosk something to pawn something. □ *Why did you ever think to mosk that?* □ *He had no money and had to mosk something.*

Mother Hubbard a cupboard. (Rhyming slang.) □ *What do you have in that Mother Hubbard?* □ *She looked in the Mother Hubbard but it was empty.*

mother of pearl a wife. (Rhyming slang, linked as follows: mother of pearl ≈ [girl] = wife.) □ *Will your mother of pearl let you out to the pub tonight?* □ *I'd better ask me mother of pearl.*

mother's ruin gin. □ *The bottle was empty. More mother's ruin, I think!* □ *Get out the mother's ruin, and let's have a drink.*

motor 1. a motor car. □ *Like my new motor, darling?* □ *I'm rather partial to fast motors.* **2.** to get along excellently; to proceed without trouble; to make good progress. □ *Look at them. Are they not really motoring?* □ *Well, we're really motoring now. It shouldn't take so long to get there.*

mouldies copper coins. □ *He chucked her a few mouldies and left.* □ *Sorry, I don't have any mouldies with me. Can you pay?*

Mozart intoxicated due to drink. (Crude. Rhyming slang, linked as follows: Mozart [and Liszt] ≈ [pissed] = intoxicated. Compare with **booed and hissed** and **Brahms and Liszt**.) □ *The hostess was really Mozart.* □ *My Mozart friend here needs a lift, and can I have one, too?*

Mrs Duckett a bucket. (Rhyming slang.) □ *Bring your Mrs Duckett over here and fill it with water.* □ *Someone has helped himself to my Mrs Duckett.*

Mrs Greenfield a place to sleep in the open. □ *Here's my Mrs Greenfield for tonight.* □ *This looks like a likely Mrs Greenfield.*

Mrs Mop(p) a nickname for a cleaning lady. □ *I was at the office so late, I met the Mrs Mop coming in as I was leaving.* □ *The Mrs Mopp we have here does not do a very great job, you know!*

muck about AND **muck around 1.** to fool around. □ *We'll muck around for a while, then get over there.* □ *That's enough mucking about for now, you two.* **2.** to potter about. □ *Instead of mucking about, could you try working for a change?* □ *Look, you can't just muck around like this all the time.*

muck around See muck about.

mucker 1. a bad fall. □ *My aunt took a mucker last week and is in hospital.* □ *Take care in there, it's easy to trip and have a mucker.* **2.** a fellow worker. □ *What are your muckers like there?* □ *I work on my own. I have no muckers.* **3.** a pal; a friend. □ *Who's your mucker, Albert?* □ *The two muckers left the pub, each one preventing the other from falling over.*

muck in (with something) to share equally in something, especially work or a task. □ *We all mucked in together and soon had the tent erected.* □ *The sooner we all muck in with this, the sooner we can all go home.*

muck something out to clean out something. □ *The farmer mucked out the cowshed every day.* □ *Right you lot! Today is the day you muck out your rooms.*

muck something up to make a mess of something; to ruin something. □ *Try not to muck things up this time.* □ *You seem to have mucked up this one, too.*

muck sweat a heavy sweat. □ *Yes it was really hard physical work, and that's why I have this muck sweat.* □ *Don't get worked up into a muck sweat over this.*

the **muesli belt** where middle-class food-faddists live. □ *They live in the muesli belt.* □ *If they are in the muesli belt, they can't be too near the poverty line.*

muggins See mug (punter).

muggo a cup or mug of tea. (Compare with **cuppa**.) □ *A muggo is always welcome.* □ *I sat down and had a lovely muggo.*

mug (punter) AND **muggins** a swindler's name for his victim. □ *I don't want to be anyone's mug punter.* □ *The con men found a handy muggins and started their scheme.*

mug's game a foolish or pointless activity. □ *Using drugs is a mug's game.* □ *Why do you fall for every mug's game going?*

mug up to learn by rapid, intensive study. □ *If you studied regularly all the time, you wouldn't need to mug at the last moment like this.* □ *She spent the night mugging up for the test.*

murg a telegram. (Backslang, from *(tele)gram*.) □ *I don't like getting no murg.* □ *Folks around here still remember murgs bringing bad news during the War.*

mushy peas boiled and mashed peas. □ *Mushy peas are particularly popular in northern England.* □ *A portion of fish and chips with mushy peas, please.*

muskra a policeman. □ *Think about how the muskra on the beat is affected by this cold.* □ *The muskra stopped at the door, tried the lock, and moved on.*

mutter and stutter See cough and stutter.

muzzy 1. befuddled due to drink. □ *Harry's a bit muzzy. As usual.* □ *Drink enough, you'll get muzzy.* **2.** dull, uninspiring, or poorly thought out. □ *Marvin is not really muzzy. He just looks, behaves, and talks that way.* □ *You can be so muzzy without even trying.*

N

nadgers small problems or difficulties. (Always plural.) □ *Where are all these nadgers coming from?* □ *They say nadgers come out of the woodwork.*

nadgery a place where **nadgers** happen. □ *Oh no, not another problem. This place is such a nadgery!* □ *Every time I go to that nadgery something else goes wrong.*

naff 1. unfashionable; tasteless; shoddy. □ *This place is really naff. Let's get out of here.* □ *Oh, what a naff weirdo!* **2.** useless. □ *Get out of here, you naff clot!* □ *I don't think he's naff at all.*

naff all See jack all.

nana a foolish person. (An abbreviation of *banana*, which is used the same way.) □ *I felt like such a bloody nana when I found out that I'd got onto the wrong train.* □ *Who's the nana in the bright orange trousers?*

nanny a boat. (Rhyming slang, linked as follows: nanny [goat] ≈ boat.) □ *Three men sat in the nanny out there for hours, fishing.* □ *We sailed out into the middle of the bay in the little nanny.*

nanny state a welfare state. □ *The over-protective nanny state is sometimes blamed for suppressing initiative.* □ *It is disparaging to call the state social security system a nanny state.*

nantee AND **nantwas** absolutely nothing. □ *Nice words, but worth nantee.* □ *We've got nantwas for you here. Shove off.*

nantwas See nantee.

nap hand a situation that justifies an expectation of winning. □ *This looks good! We've a nap hand here, I think.* □ *Remember telling us we had a nap hand? Well, the other side has won.*

napoo something that either does not exist or is of no use whatsoever. (Said to be an abbreviation of the French *il n'y en a plus*, meaning "there is no more of it." If so, this is an example of hobson-jobson.) □ *Forget it. It's napoo.* □ *It may be napoo to you, but that does not mean it's unimportant to someone else.*

napper the head. □ *He's distinctive because he has a particularly large napper.* □ *Turn your napper around and take a look at this.*

narked annoyed or angered. □ *Just walk away. Don't let him cause you to become narked.* □ *Now that gets me really narked, you know.*

narky AND **sarky** sarcastic. (Narky is rhyming slang from sarky.) □ *There's no need to be narky.* □ *I'm not being sarky.*

nasty piece of work an unpleasant person. (Offensive. Also a term of address.) □ *Just get out of my sight, you nasty piece of work!* □ *What a nasty piece of work you are!*

natty admirable; attractive; neat. □ *That's a natty suit.* □ *We've got a natty way to solve that problem.*

natural 1. someone with obvious natural talent or skill in some activity or other. □ *That guy is a natural!* □ *Brother, can she dance! What a natural!* **2.** one's lifespan. □ *In all my natural, I never thought I'd see that!* □ *She spent her entire natural living in that one small village.*

nauticals haemorrhoids. (Taboo. Rhyming slang, linked as follows: nautical [mile]s ≈ [piles] = haemorrhoids.) □ *The wife's got the nauticals and is in a foul mood.* □ *She's got to go into hospital to get her nauticals dealt with.*

navvy a nautical or aerial navigator. □ *Ask the navvy where we are!* □ *He's the navvy on a jumbo jet.*

near and far a car. (Rhyming slang.) □ *I'm rather partial to nears and fars.* □ *Like my new near and far, darling?*

near (to) the knuckle See close to the knuckle.

neaters a drink of neat spirits. □ *Sam usually has one or two neaters on the way home.* □ *I'll take a neaters—just the way it is now.*

neck See brass neck.

neddy a donkey. □ *There's a sanctuary for old and ill neddies near here.* □ *The kids went for a ride on a neddy along the seashore.*

the **needful** money. □ *Sorry, I can't afford it, I've not enough of the needful.* □ *How much of the needful do you need, then?*

needle and pin gin. (Rhyming slang.) □ *Can I have a needle and pin, please?* □ *I do like this needle and pin.*

needle and thread bread. (Rhyming slang.) □ *Even a few slices of needle and thread would be good.* □ *Any needle and thread, love?*

needle fight AND **needle game; needle match** a contest or game where the outcome is important and finely balanced. □ *What do think will happen at the needle fight tonight?* □ *The needle match has gone into extra time, so it must be close.*

needle game See needle fight.

needle match See needle fight.

needle something from someone to prise information from someone. □ *I wish you would stop trying to needle that information from me.* □ *I'm afraid there's nothing to needle from him.*

negative capital debt. (A euphemism.) □ *There is the small matter of our negative capital.* □ *Unfortunately all we have to our name is, well, negative capital.*

Nellie Blight an eye. (Rhyming slang, linked as follows: Nellie Blight ≈ [sight] = eye.) □ *I think there's something wrong with me Nellie Blights.* □ *He looked me right in the Nellie Blight and assured me again that he was telling the truth.*

Newingtons the abdomen. (Rhyming slang, linked as follows: Newington [Butts] ≈ [guts] = abdomen. Newington Butts is a road in south London.) □ *Cor! I've been kicked right in the Newingtons!* □ *He's got some bug in the Newingtons but I'm sure he'll be okay in a day or so.*

new penny the penny that has been in circulation since decimalisation of the currency in 1971. (It is worth ¹⁄₁₀₀th of a pound.) □ *What can you buy for one new penny?* □ *You get very little for a new penny, but even less for an old penny.*

the **News of the Screws** the *News of the World*, a Sunday newspaper published in London which is famous for the extensive coverage it gives to sexual matters. (Crude.) □ *Sunday morning, and time to buy the latest News of the Screws.* □ *The News of the Screws is a source of endless harmless titillation across the land.*

newted See pissed as a newt.

next (door) but one following the next; two ahead. □ *These people don't live in the house next door but next door but one.* □ *We're next but one after the greengrocer's.*

nick 1. the state or condition of something. □ *What sort of nick is it in?* □ *We must know what nick he's in before we know what to do.* **2.** the **nick** a police station. □ *Right, let's get you to the nick.* □ *I don't want to go to the nick!* **3.** the **nick** a jail. □ *Welcome to the nick. Now, strip!* □ *If you're looking for Otto, try the nick.*

nicker one pound sterling. (The plural is the same.) □ *These things cost more than just a few nicker?* □ *Have you got a few nicker you can spare?*

nick off to play truant, especially from school. □ *By the time the class resumed after lunch, almost half the pupils appeared to have nicked off.* □ *Where are the children nicking off to, the teacher wondered?*

niff 1. a bad smell. □ *I just can't stand that niff.* □ *Where is that terrible niff coming from?* **2.** to emit a bad smell; to stink. □ *The food, which had been left to rot, niffed in a most offensive manner.* □ *The fact is, the tramp was niffing badly.*

niffy smelly. □ *If you must be niffy, be so somewhere else thank you.* □ *That's really niffy, don't go in there.*

ninepence to the shilling lacking intelligence or common sense; simple-minded. (In pre-1971 currency, there were 12 pennies in one shilling.) □ *Yes, clearly he's ninepence to the shilling.* □ *He may be ninepence to the shilling, but he's a really nice person.*

nitty foolish. □ *Don't be nitty. That's impossible.* □ *That was a nitty idea.*

n.o. not out. (In cricket.) □ *No, it's an n.o.* □ *Oh surely the umpire can't call that one another n.o.*

Noah's ark 1. the dark. (Rhyming slang.) □ *It usually is Noah's ark in the country at night when the moon's not up.* □ *It's really Noah's ark out there, you know.* **2.** a park. (Rhyming slang.) □ *I like being able to look out over the Noah's ark from my flat.* □ *After lunch, we went for a stroll in the Noah's ark.* **3.** an informer. (Rhyming slang, linked as follows: Noah's ark ≈ [nark] = informer.) □ *This new Noah's ark gives me good info.* □ *I don't trust Noah's arks.*

nob 1. a wealthy or high-class person. □ *Here was one nob that was different from the others, he thought.* □ *I don't think I could take another nob like that today.* **2.** the head. □ *Harry's distinctive hairy nob hove into view.* □ *Where'd you get that nasty bump on your nob?*

nobble 1. to acquire money by dishonest means. □ *I wonder how he nobbled that money.* □ *If you nobble money, sooner or later someone will nobble you.* **2.** to catch or arrest a criminal. (Police.) □ *If I'm nobbled, I'll get ten years.* □ *The police nobbled him as he went to buy a newspaper.* **3.** to secure support by cheating. □ *Somehow or other she nobbled their support away from me.* □ *Right, can we do this without any nobbling this time?* **4.** to tamper with a racehorse to prevent it from winning. □ *I think someone must have nobbled the favourite.* □ *Why would anyone want to nobble that horse?* **5.** to influence or attempt to influence a jury or an individual member of a jury. □ *If they catch you trying to nobble the jury they'll throw away the key.* □ *Nobbling is a very serious offence.*

no cop useless. □ *Sorry, that computer is no cop.* □ *All of them were no cop, as it turned out.*

noddle 1. the head. □ *That's using your noddle.* □ *Put your hat on your noddle, and let's go.* **2.** a fool or half-wit. (Use with caution. Also a term of address.) □ *Martin can be a complete noddle at times.* □ *Ignore them, Mary. These boys are just noddles.*

noddy a police officer on foot patrol. (From the name of a well-known nursery character made of wood, who nods his head when speaking.) □ *The burglar was caught red-handed by the local noddy.* □ *What does the noddy want?*

noddy bike a small, underpowered motorcycle once used by police officers. □ *I saw a copper on a noddy bike the other day.* □ *Naw. The police haven't used noddy bikes for years.*

noddy car a small car. □ *I need a car, not a big one. A noddy car would do.* □ *You look ridiculous in that noddy car.*

noel a coward. (Based on the name of playwright Noel Coward.) □ *Well, are we all just noels, or are we going to do this?* □ *I knew it, you're just a noel like all the rest.*

no-hoper 1. a hopeless case. □ *He's a total no-hoper, I'm sorry to say.* □ *Harry has become a no-hoper.* **2.** a person lacking the ability, drive, or opportunity necessary to succeed. □ *What does the no-hoper want?* □ *Even a no-hoper like that has to earn a living.*

no joy a failure. □ *Sorry, no joy.* □ *It's true. It was no joy again.*

none too clever See *not so clever.*

none too smart See *not so clever.*

no oil painting an ugly person. (Offensive.) □ *Bert's no oil painting, that's for sure.* □ *OK, I agree she's no oil painting, but she does have a lovely personality.*

north and south the mouth. (Rhyming slang.) □ *Have I ever told you that you have an ugly north and south?* □ *Shut your north and south and get on with your work.*

North Countryman a male native, citizen, or inhabitant of northern England. □ *I'm a North Countryman and don't take to your soft southern ways.* □ *North Countrymen can seem gruff, but really they are very kind and helpful.*

nose 1. a criminal's informant. (Underworld.) □ *My nose told me about you.* □ *Mr Big has many noses.* **2.** to spy. □ *I think there's someone nosing around outside the house.* □ *If you want to nose in my business, why not just ask? I've no secrets.*

nose and chin to win. (Rhyming slang.) □ *Sally nosed and chinned in the lottery.* □ *He's convinced he'll nose and chin the big prize.*

nose-to-tail [of traffic] closely packed together. □ *The traffic was nose-to-tail on the by-pass this morning.* □ *I've been stuck in this nose-to-tail stuff for hours.*

nosh 1. to eat. (From the German *naschen*, meaning "to nibble," via Yiddish.) □ *You nosh too much.* □ *Every time I see you, you're noshing.* **2.** food. □ *How about some nosh?* □ *It's lunchtime. Let's go and find some nosh.*

nosher a greedy person. □ *Even a nosher like that has to earn a living.* □ *What does the nosher want?*

noshery a restaurant. □ *Do you know a good Indian noshery around here?* □ *There's a good noshery down the street so you won't starve.*

nosh-up a big meal. □ *That was a great nosh-up at Tom's the other night.* □ *I haven't had a nosh-up like that in years.*

not a bean without any money. □ *Me? Lend you money? I've not a bean.* □ *I had not a bean by the end of the week, but it was well worth it.*

not a bleeding thing AND **not a blind thing; not a dicky (bird); not a sausage** absolutely nothing. (Not a dicky (bird) is rhyming slang, linked as follows: not a dicky (bird) ≈ [not a word] = [silence] = nothing.) □ *Sorry, this story is not a bleeding thing to* *do with me, all right?* □ *Say nothing, not a dicky bird.* □ *Okay, not a sausage, mate.*

not a blind thing See not a bleeding thing.

not a dicky (bird) See not a bleeding thing.

not a sausage See not a bleeding thing.

not before time late; at last. □ *Well, there you are—and not before time!* □ *Not before time, he got the situation back under control.*

not bothered AND **not fussy** unconcerned; indifferent. □ *She seems to be not bothered by his fate.* □ *This is what you get for the money. I'm not fussy whether you like it or not.*

notch something up AND **tote something up** to count up something; to add up or score something. □ *Well, it looks like we notched up another victory.* □ *The crooks were able to tote up just one more theft before they were caught.*

not for toffee under no circumstances. □ *No, not for toffee!* □ *I would not go there, not for toffee.*

not fussy See not bothered.

not go much on someone to dislike someone, somewhat. □ *You don't go much on her, do you?* □ *The plain truth is she does not go much on her.*

nothing loath willing. □ *Well, nothing loath, here goes!* □ *Certainly he has a very nothing loath attitude.*

not long arrived AND **not long here** newly arrived. □ *We're not long arrived and don't yet know our way around.* □ *They have not long here so show them what to do, where to go, and so on.*

not long here See not long arrived.

not much cop of little use. □ *Simon's not much cop when it comes to thinking, I'm afraid.* □ *The original idea was not much cop so we've come up with another.*

not on not acceptable; not possible. □ *I'm afraid that's just not on.* □ *What you suggest is not on. Please come up with an acceptable alternative.*

not short of a bob or two prosperous. □ *Oh yes, he's not short of a bob or two.* □ *Anyone who can afford a house like that must be not short of a bob or two.*

not so clever AND **not very clever; not too clever; none too clever; not so smart; not very smart; none too smart; not too smart 1.** unwell. □ *Mike's not so clever this morning, but I think he'll be well again soon.* □ *Oh dear, I feel not so smart today.* □ *She took ill at work and was still not too clever by the time she got home.* □ *Carol is none too smart today, I'm afraid.* **2.** unlikeable; unpleasant. □ *Well, the weather was not very clever over the weekend, was it?* □ *Letting yourself turn into a drug addict is none too clever—and it's not very smart either.* **3.** broken; unusable. □ *The TV set's not so clever today. We'll have to get it fixed.* □ *Oh dear, the computer's not so smart today.* □ *Maggie's car was not looking too clever after she drove it into that tree.*

not so dusty just about acceptable. □ *Well all right, that's not so dusty I suppose.* □ *Try to keep things not so dusty.*

not so smart See not so clever.

not take a blind bit of notice of someone or something to completely disregard someone or something; to deliberately ignore someone or something. □ *My advice to you is to not take a blind bit of notice of the defect and the chances are no one else will either.* □ *Are you deliberately not taking a blind bit of notice of me in the hope I'll go away?*

not too clever See not so clever.

not too smart See not so clever.

not very clever See not so clever.

not very smart See not so clever.

nuppence no money. □ *I'm broke. I've nuppence!* □ *Nuppence is all I'd pay for that thing.*

nut-rock a bald person. □ *He's a pleasant nut-rock.* □ *The nut-rock was waiting outside the office for him.*

oak to fool around. (Rhyming slang, linked as follows: oak ≈ [joke] = fool around.) ☐ *Stop oaking and start working.* ☐ *Their kids just oak around all day.*

obie man a burglar who reads obituaries so that he knows which houses will be empty while the occupants are attending a funeral. ☐ *Otto thought being an obie man was smart.* ☐ *Unfortunately, Otto discovered that to be an obie man you have to be able to read.*

ocean wave a shave. (Rhyming slang.) ☐ *I need an ocean wave.* ☐ *He asked the barber to give him an ocean wave.*

odds and sods miscellaneous items. ☐ *Why do you never sort out these odds and sods?* ☐ *There's an even bigger pile of odds and sods over there in that corner.*

off by heart memorised; known by heart. ☐ *In my day we had to learn our tables off by heart.* ☐ *Some people still think learning off by heart is the best way to learn.*

off colour in poor health. ☐ *Carol is a bit off colour today, I'm afraid.* ☐ *Oh dear, I feel rather off colour.*

off form performing worse than usual. (Compare with on form.) ☐ *That was terrible! She must be off form tonight.* ☐ *Try not to be off form again tomorrow.*

off one's block See off one's chump.

off one's chump AND **off one's rocker; off one's trolley; off one's block; off one's head; off one's nut; off the chump; off the crust; off the head; off the scone** crazy; insane; eccentric. ☐ *Just ignore Uncle Charles. He's off his chump.* ☐ *Am I off my trolley, or did that car suddenly disappear?* ☐ *You must really be off the crust if you think I'll put up with that kind of stuff.*

off one's head See off one's chump.

off one's nut See off one's chump.

off one's rocker See *off one's chump*.

off one's trolley See *off one's chump*.

off the chump See *off one's chump*.

off the crust See *off one's chump*.

off the head See *off one's chump*.

off-the-peg [of clothes] ready-made. □ *We came across this shop selling nothing but off-the-peg dresses.* □ *Only common people wear off-the-peg clothes, Mother!*

off the scone See *off one's chump*.

oi(c)k an uncultured or boorish person; a country yokel. □ *What's an oick like that doing around here?* □ *I'm sorry but we really don't need another oik working here.*

oil the knocker to bribe or to tip a doorman. □ *Why do you want to oil the knocker?* □ *I'm sure you can oil the knocker of at least one doorman, if you try hard enough.*

oily lamp a tramp. (Rhyming slang.) □ *Even a oily lamp like that needs some money.* □ *The oily lamp was waiting outside the office for him.*

oily rag 1. an incompetent car mechanic. □ *Where's that oily rag friend of yours who serviced my car so it's worse than before he started, then?* □ *I would not say Joe's an oily rag. Not the world's greatest car mechanic, yes. But not an oily rag, no.* **2.** a cigarette. (Rhyming slang, linked as follows: oily rag ≈ [fag] = cigarette.) □ *Hey, mate, gimme an oily rag.* □ *Go and buy your own oily rags!*

old and bitter a mother-in-law. (A pun on mild and bitter.) □ *I'll ask my old and bitter if I can go.* □ *What time does your old and bitter get home?*

the Old Bill the police. □ *Get away, get away! The Old Bill are outside!* □ *The Old Bill are after me!*

old bubble a wife. (Rhyming slang, linked as follows: old bubble ≈ [trouble (and strife)] ≈ wife. Compare with **trouble and strife**.) □ *I've got to go home to my old bubble.* □ *My old bubble disapproved of the film.*

(old) buffer a foolish but harmless old man. □ *There's an old buffer asking for you at the door.* □ *That poor buffer thinks he can convince them.*

old King Cole the dole. (Rhyming slang.) □ *I'm off to collect my old King Cole.* □ *How long have you been on the old King Cole now?*

old lag 1. a habitual convict. □ *An old lag has certain informal privileges denied to new prisoners.* □ *All the old lags are kept in that wing.* **2.** a former convict. □ *You'd never guess Charlie's an old lag, would you?* □ *Watch out, he's an old lag, you know.*

old Mick nauseous; sick. (Rhyming slang.) □ *Paul was feeling a bit of the old Mick so he went home.* □ *If you're old Mick, we better stop.*

old sweat 1. an old soldier. □ *Old sweats, like old soldiers, never die. They just fade away.* □ *Who's the old sweat sitting in the corner?* **2.** an experienced individual. □ *Don't worry, he's an old sweat. John'll be all right with him.* □ *I suppose I'm a bit of an old sweat, having been working here for over twenty years now.*

old trout an unpleasant old woman. □ *Please get that old trout out of here!* □ *This old trout is looking for work, I think.*

oliver a fist. (Rhyming slang, linked as follows: Oliver [Twist] ≈ fist. Oliver Twist was a character in Dickens's novel of the same name.) □ *Put up your olivers, you young whippersnapper!* □ *His olivers were about twice the size of mine!*

once (and) for all See for good and all.

oncer 1. impudence. (Rhyming slang, linked as follows: oncer = [once a week] ≈ [cheek] = impudence.) □ *What a oncer that is! Who does that woman think she is?* □ *Any more oncers like that and he'll get everything he deserves.* **2.** a unique person, object, or event. □ *The oncer was still waiting outside the office for him.* □ *He really is a oncer.*

one-and-one a portion of fish and chips suitable for one person. (Irish usage.) □ *That's him over there, eating the one-and-one.* □ *Do you sell one-and-ones in here, love?*

one and t'other 1. brother. (Rhyming slang.) □ *Can I bring me one and t'other?* □ *Terry's here, and he's brought his one and t'other with him.* **2.** mother. (Rhyming slang.) □ *I'd better ask me one and t'other.* □ *Will your one and t'other let you out to the pub tonight?*

on form AND **on song** performing as expected; performing well. (Compare with off form.) □ *When she's on form she's the best there is.* □ *Wonderful! She really was on song tonight.*

on offer for sale at a reduced price. □ *I see his car's on offer now.* □ *I'm looking for a bargain—one that's on offer.*

on one's Jack (Jones) alone. (Rhyming slang.) □ *Since Mary left me, I've been on my Jack Jones.* □ *I'll be coming along on my Jack, I'm afraid.*

on pins nervous or agitated. □ *When I get on pins, I meditate.* □ *Sally was really on pins before the meeting.*

on song See on form.

on suss on suspicion. □ *You're arresting me on suss! Nothing more!* □ *You can't arrest people on nothing but suss.*

on tap immediately available. (From beer available on tap.) □ *By coincidence, I have on tap just the kind of person you're talking about.* □ *The cook has any kind of food you might want on tap.*

on the boil 1. busily active. □ *Things are really on the boil at the factory.* □ *Those teenagers are always on the boil!* **2.** requiring urgent attention. □ *Come on! This thing is really on the boil now!* □ *Once the process gets on the boil, you can't leave it.*

on the cards probable. □ *Yes, it's on the cards. It could happen.* □ *I had never thought such a thing was on the cards.*

on the fiddle working a swindle. □ *I'm sure Harry's on the fiddle again.* □ *At least Otto's too thick to be on the fiddle. Isn't he?*

on the floor poor. (Rhyming slang.) □ *Since the factory closed, everyone in this town is on the floor.* □ *No, I can't lend you money. I'm on the floor myself.*

on the knocker selling from door to door. □ *There's someone here on the knocker.* □ *I see Harry's on the knocker nowadays.*

on the (lifting) game engaging in stealing. □ *Otto's on the game again, stealing whatever he can find.* □ *I am not on the lifting game, Inspector!*

on the mains connected to the public electricity supply. □ *Of course we're on the mains! Where do you think this is? Outer Mongolia?* □ *Even remote parts of Scotland have been on the mains for over fifty years, you know.*

on the mike with nothing to do. □ *He's just hanging around, on the mike.* □ *They'll just have to stay on the mike until this is over.*

on the never-never purchasing by hire purchase, on the instalment plan. □ *Buying things on the never-never is always expensive.* □ *We bought the new car on the never-never, you know.*

on the nod agreed without comment. □ *There's no way that'll get passed on the nod.* □ *In the end, the scheme was agreed on the nod!*

on the phone 1. connected to the telephone system. □ *Yes, I'm on the phone. Here's my number.* □ *If you're on the phone there, perhaps I could call you?* **2.** speaking on the telephone. □ *She's on the phone but won't be long.* □ *Please take a seat while I'm on the phone.*

on the ramp participating in or conducting a swindle. □ *Are you on the ramp, too?* □ *The police are looking for a couple on some sort of ramp involving visiting old folks in this area.*

on the razzle having a good time. □ *They're out on the razzle again.* □ *Come on, let's go on the razzle!*

on the square belonging to a Masonic lodge. □ *I hear the police superintendent is on the square.* □ *Are you on the square, Albert?*

on the strap purchasing by hire purchase, on the instalment plan. □ *We bought the new car on the strap, you know.* □ *Buying things on the strap is always expensive.*

on the strength 1. on the payroll. □ *Right, you're on the strength.* □ *I was hoping to get on the strength here.* **2.** a member of the team. □ *Well, welcome aboard. Now you're on the strength.* □ *Everyone on the strength will have to help.*

on the thumb hitchhiking. □ *I think it's too dangerous to travel on the thumb nowadays.* □ *A couple of teenagers on the thumb were standing at the next intersection.*

on the trot 1. busily occupied. □ *I'll talk to you later when I'm not so much on the trot.* □ *I was on the trot and couldn't get to the phone.* **2.** in rapid succession. □ *Why are all these things happening on the trot like this?* □ *I've got a whole lot of things to attend to on the trot today.*

on the whine complaining. □ *There you are, always on the whine.* □ *I would be surprised if she was not on the whine.*

oof cash. (This is derived from *ooftisch*, a Yiddish term derived from the German *auf (dem) Tische*, meaning "on (the) table" in English. In other words, **oof** is money actually placed on the table—which is to say, cash.) □ *I don't make enough oof to go on a trip like that!* □ *It takes a lot of oof to buy a car like that.*

oofy rich. (From **oof**.) □ *The Wilmington-Thorpes are oofy.* □ *Well, what do you think? He won the lottery and of course he's oofy.*

oppo an associate or colleague. □ *This is Harry. He's my oppo.* □ *Your oppo phoned. There's a problem at your office.*

orbital a party occurring just outside London. (In other words, just beyond the M25 motorway, which "orbits" London.) □ *Sam invited us to an orbital, but we're getting a little old for that kind of thing.* □ *Fred knows how to put on a real orbital!*

the **order of the boot** AND the **order of the wellie 1.** a dismissal; a rejection. □ *I've just been given the order of the boot.* □ *Shape up fast, or it's the order of the wellie for you, son.* **2.** a job dismissal; the sack. □ *Give him the order of the boot. He's no use.* □ *The firm just gave me the order of the wellie!*

order of the wellie See order of the boot.

outer a convenient explanation for why something went wrong; an excuse. □ *This outer that we have all been getting from Kevin is just too much.* □ *I listened to her outer without saying anything.*

over the moon very pleased indeed. □ *She was over the moon when she heard the news.* □ *I did point out that it was a bit soon to be over the moon. There was still work to be done.*

over the road AND **over the way** upon the other side of the street. □ *She waved to her friend over the road.* □ *Over the way she could see the shop she was looking for.*

over the way See over the road.

Oxbridge Oxford and Cambridge taken together; what they have in common. (Compare with **Camford**.) □ *There is a sort of Oxbridge mentality which some think is bad for British business.* □ *I don't know whether he went to Oxford or Cambridge, but it was one or the other. Let's just settle for Oxbridge, eh?*

Oxford twenty-five pence; previously five shillings. (Rhyming slang, linked as follows: Oxford [scholar] ≈ [dollar] = five shillings. This originated in the 19th century, when £1 = $4 for a great many years, so that five shillings equaled $1.00.) □ *Thanks for the Oxford, guv.* □ *An Oxford? Is that all?*

P

P AND **p; pee** a penny; a new penny. (Since decimalisation in 1971.) □ *That will cost you five P, mate.* □ *Have you got twenty pee on you?*

pack in AND **pack up 1.** [for people] to give up. □ *Why did you pack in just as it was starting to work?* □ *Oh, he packed up long ago.* **2.** [for machines] to cease to function. □ *My computer packed in today.* □ *The car packed up halfway here.* **3.** to retire; to cease to be employed. □ *Well, I'll soon be 65 and it'll be time to pack in.* □ *I want to pack up well before I'm 65, if I can.*

pack out somewhere to fill some venue or event completely with people. □ *They certainly managed to pack out that reception!* □ *If they pack out the theatre they'll make a fortune.*

pack someone or something in See jack someone or something in.

pack up See pack in.

Paddy's taxi a police car. □ *Watch it! That's a Paddy's taxi!* □ *The Paddy's taxi drove forward, blocking my exit.*

paddy(wack) a burst of anger or excitement. □ *Don't start another paddywack, or you'll get fired.* □ *Otto really had a terrible paddy when he was told.*

pad the hoof to walk. □ *Stop padding the hoof long enough to eat some dinner.* □ *I padded the hoof all day, looking for a present for Sarah.*

panda (car) a police patrol car, called this because of broad white stripes reminiscent of the panda. □ *The panda drove past slowly, but did not stop.* □ *Mike ran out into the road to wave down the panda.*

pan-flasher a short-lived success; someone or something that is a flash in the pan. □ *It was all right but really no more than a pan-flasher.* □ *We don't need pan-flashers, but real successes.*

panhandler a hospital orderly. □ *Ask the panhandler to help.* □ *I'm a panhandler in the hospital.*

pantomime absurd or outrageous behaviour. □ *The whole episode rapidly turned into a pantomime.* □ *Right, that's enough of this pantomime!*

paraffin budgie a helicopter. □ *I never want to fly in a paraffin budgie. Those things scare me.* □ *See that paraffin budgie up there? It's measuring your driving speed. Slow down.*

park a custard to empty one's stomach; to vomit. (Crude.) □ *Harry is in the loo parking a custard.* □ *Who parked a custard on the floor?*

parky bitterly cold. (Particularly with reference to mornings, the air, etc.) □ *Cor! Real parky today, innit?* □ *In parky weather like this he prefers to stay indoors.*

pash a childish passion or infatuation. □ *She's always having a pash for some pop idol or other.* □ *These pashes are becoming serious, I fear.*

pass a comment to comment. □ *All I did was to pass a comment on her new dress.* □ *If you want to pass a comment, check it with me first, please.*

past it unable to continue because of age. □ *Old Willie is clearly past it, I'm afraid.* □ *Once you're past it, you should retire.*

patches pieces sewn onto a prisoner's uniform. □ *Prisoners' uniforms have patches to enable easy identification in the event of escape.* □ *Is that the police? There's a man wearing patches trying to hide at the bottom of our garden.*

pay round a recurring discussion about pay between trade union and employer. □ *Time for the annual pay round again, I think.* □ *How much of a fight do you expect during this pay round?*

PC a police constable. □ *PCs are responsible for upholding the law.* □ *My brother Nigel is a PC.*

pea-brained stupid. □ *Whoever was the pea-brained clown who came up with that moronic idea?* □ *Tom has nothing upstairs. If you prefer, he's pea-brained.*

pear-shaped out of control; wrong. □ *My stereo's gone pear-shaped again.* □ *I'm afraid my car's steering's gone pear-shaped. It's too dangerous to drive.*

peas hot. (Rhyming slang, linked as follows: peas [in the pot] ≈ hot.) □ *I can't take another peas day like this.* □ *Cor, it's really peas in there!*

pecker the mouth. □ *Put this in your pecker and chew it up.* □ *Shut your pecker!*

pee See P.

penguin suit See claw-hammer suit.

pennif a banknote. (Backslang of finnip, hence a five pound note, hence any banknote.) □ *Sorry, I don't have any pennifs with me. Can you pay?* □ *He put a number of pennifs into the top pocket of my shirt and said that there were plenty more to be had if I asked no questions.*

penn'orth (of chalk) AND **ball o' chalk; ball of chalk** a walk. (Rhyming slang.) □ *Go on! Get out! Take a penn'orth!* □ *I went for a ball of chalk, just to get away from him.*

penny a smile. (Rhyming slang, linked as follows: penny[-a-mile] ≈ smile.) □ *Was that a penny?* □ *What a pretty penny she has.*

the **penny drops** finally there is understanding. □ *At last, the penny drops.* □ *Eventually the penny drops and we are able to move on.*

penny steamboat a ferry. □ *We crossed the Channel on one of these penny steamboats.* □ *I think they're trying to tell us that the penny steamboat is ready to leave, Sir.*

Period! See Full stop!

perisher an irritating person, especially a child. □ *She's an infuriating little perisher.* □ *If you can't control that perisher of yours, you can't stay here.*

perishing 1. extremely cold. □ *I know it's perishing out, but someone has to do it.* □ *In perishing weather like this, I try to avoid going outdoors.* **2.** confounded. □ *The perishing thing is broken.* □ *That is a perishing nuisance.*

phone through AND **ring through; ring up** to call on the telephone. □ *I'll just phone through now.* □ *You'd better ring up to find out what she wants.*

(physical) jerks physical exercises. □ *Do we have to participate in these physical jerks every morning?* □ *He takes about ten minutes of jerks every day before breakfast.*

pi pious. □ Why does he always have to be so darned pi? □ Do you find that pi people like that make you suspicious?

pick and choose beer or spirits. (Rhyming slang, linked as follows: pick and choose ≈ [booze] = beer/spirits.) □ Here, that's good pick and choose! □ Have a can of pick and choose, Charlie.

pickle a troublesome child. □ Is this pickle yours? □ She is a most irritating pickle.

pie and liquor a clergyman. (Rhyming slang, linked as follows: pie and liquor ≈ [vicar] = clergyman.) □ I went to see the pie and liquor for some advice. □ Most of the time, pie and liquors don't seem to have much to do.

piffy unlikely; improbable; suspect. □ It's really piffy, but if you think so, OK. □ That is a really piffy suggestion. It's absurd!

pig 1. someone who eats too much; a glutton. (Offensive, but sometimes jocular.) □ Stop being a pig! Save some for other people. □ I try to cut down on calories, but whenever I see red meat I make a pig of myself. **2.** a dirty or slovenly person. (Offensive.) □ Max is a pig. I don't think he bathes enough. □ Jimmy, change your clothes. Look at that mud, you little pig! **3.** a police officer. (Offensive. Although widely known only since the 1960s, this sense of the word was in fact quite common in 19th-century London.) □ The pig did break up the fight. □ These two pigs drove around in their pigmobile aggravating innocent people like me. **4.** a rugby football. □ He grabbed the pig as it flew out of the scrum and ran with it all the way. □ He hoisted the pig with one fine kick right over the cross-bar. **5.** a portion of an orange. □ She peeled and opened up the orange, offering each of us a pig. □ He took each pig, one by one, and swallowed it whole.

piggery AND **pigsty** a house or a room that is in a filthy or slovenly condition. (Compare with **pig's breakfast**.) □ It really is a piggery, Simon. □ What a pigsty you've turned this place into!

pig-ignorant very ignorant, especially of what is acceptable social behaviour. □ Stupid? He's more like pig-ignorant, I'd say. □ Yes, he's pig-ignorant, but we need him, OK?

pig it to live in squalor. □ Without doubt, they are pigging it. □ Why do you have to pig it like this all the time?

pigs See pig's ear.

pig's arse See pig's breakfast.

pig's breakfast AND **pig's ear; pig's arse** a chaotic mess; a complete disaster; a total failure. (**Pig's arse** is taboo. Other expressions are crude. Compare with **piggery**.) □ *Why do you have to make a pig's breakfast of everything you touch?* □ *What a pig's arse this place has become.*

pig's ear 1. year. (Rhyming slang.) □ *Look, I've been working on this for a whole pig's ear and I'm fed up with it.* □ *It'll take more than one pig's ear to put that right.* **2.** See **pig's breakfast**. **3.** AND **pigs** beer. (Rhyming slang.) □ *Give my friend here a pig's ear.* □ *How about a pigs before you go, Charlie?*

pigsty See **piggery**.

pillock 1. a fool; an idiot. □ *I felt like a pillock when I found out that I'd got onto the wrong train.* □ *Those pillocks are at it again. Spend, spend, spend.* **2.** an objectionable person. □ *What a pillock you are!* □ *Just get out of my sight, you pillock!*

pill opera any TV soap opera about life in a hospital. □ *She just loves all these pill operas on the TV.* □ *There are several pill operas on tonight, dear.*

pimple a hill. □ *There's a castle on that pimple.* □ *Let's climb the pimple and look at the castle.*

pimple and blotch whisky. (Rhyming slang, linked as follows: pimple and blotch ≈ [Scotch] = whisky.) □ *The pimple and blotch was certainly flowing that evening, I can tell you.* □ *I could go a glass or three of the old pimple and blotch.*

pink 'un a newspaper, such as the *Financial Times*, that is printed upon pink paper. □ *Every morning he bought a pink 'un and read it on the train taking him to work.* □ *So why should newspapers not be pink 'uns?*

pinny an apron. (From *pinafore*.) □ *Doesn't he look sweet, standing there in his pinny!* □ *She put on her pinny and went to tidy up the house.*

pint this quantity of beer, especially as an order in a pub. □ *How about a pint?* □ *Make mine a pint, thanks.*

pinta a pint of milk. (A corruption of *pint of* invented for a campaign to encourage milk consumption in the 1960s.) □ *Ask the milkman to leave an extra pinta, please.* □ *She went into the dairy and asked for a pinta.*

pip 1. to blackball someone. □ *You can't join the club. I'm afraid you've been pipped.* □ *Why should anyone want to pip me?* **2.** to defeat someone. □ *Oh, we'll pip them.* □ *How did we get pipped again?* **3.** to hit someone or some creature with a shell from a gun. □ *The trench was pipped, killing everyone in it.* □ *I bet you can't pip that pigeon over there.* **4.** the **pip** a strong feeling of irritation or disgust. □ *That really gives me the pip.* □ *No wonder we got the pip.*

pip at the post to defeat at the very last moment. □ *We were pipped at the post.* □ *Don't try to pip them at the post.*

the **Pipe** the underground railway system of London. (Compare with Tube, which is much more commonly heard.) □ *Does the Pipe go to Crystal Palace?* □ *He likes using the Pipe because it's so quick.*

pipe one's eyes to weep. □ *When I heard, I had to pipe my eyes.* □ *Stop piping your eyes and act like a man!*

pipped annoyed. □ *The whole business got her pipped after a while.* □ *Fiona was pipped, once she realised what the remark meant.*

pissed as a newt AND **newted** very intoxicated due to drink. (Both are crude; pissed as a newt is taboo.) □ *Tipsy? Pissed as a newt, more like!* □ *Joe and Arthur kept on knocking them back till they were both completely newted.*

pit a bed. □ *Somebody put a spider in my pit.* □ *I was so tired I could hardly find my pit.*

Plain and Gravy See Lumpy Gravy.

planky dull-witted; stupid. (From *as thick as a plank.*) □ *Oh come on, he must be the plankiest person on the planet.* □ *How planky can you get?*

plates and dishes 1. kisses. (Rhyming slang. Always in the plural.) □ *Barlowe was greeted at the door by a lovely, cuddly bird in a nightie—eyes closed and lips parted for some better-than-average plates and dishes. He really wished—just for a moment—that he hadn't rung the wrong doorbell.* □ *He planted a series of quick plates and dishes square on her lips. She kicked him in the shins for his trouble.* **2.** wife. (Rhyming slang, linked as follows: plates and dishes ≈ [missus] = wife.) □ *I've got to get home to the plates and dishes.* □ *The plates and dishes is angry with me.*

plates of meat the feet. (Rhyming slang. Always plural.) □ *My plates of meat are aching after all that walking.* □ *Sit down and give your plates of meat a rest.*

play gooseberry to be a third person present when the other two wish to be alone. □ *Why must she always play gooseberry?* □ *I think Aunt Martha actually does not even realise she's playing gooseberry.*

plod 1. a uniformed police officer, especially when on foot patrol. □ *There's a plod walking down the passage towards us.* □ *Get rid of that plod before he finds out what's really going on here.* **2.** the **plod** the police force; especially the uniformed section. □ *The plod are after me!* □ *Get away, get away! The plod are outside!*

plonker 1. a big, loud, wet kiss. □ *His aunt gave him a plonker on his forehead and he cringed.* □ *Jimmy hates aunts who give their young nephews plonkers.* **2.** a stupid mistake. □ *Oh no, you've made another plonker.* □ *Any more plonkers like that and you're out!* **3.** a foolish or unimaginative person. □ *Those plonkers are at it again. Spend, spend, spend.* □ *You plonker! You've buttered the tablecloth!* **4. plonkers** the feet. □ *Sit down and give your plonkers a rest.* □ *My plonkers are aching after all that walking.*

plough to fail an academic examination. □ *I ploughed history again.* □ *I ploughed all my exams except history.*

plummy of a form of affected speech which sounds as if the speaker has a plum in his or her mouth. □ *Who's the geezer with the plummy accent on the phone?* □ *Some people might say your voice is plummy, you know.*

poach to recruit someone by enticing him or her away from a current employer. □ *Someone's poaching our best workers.* □ *Can you poach any more people from the other factory?*

podged replete; too full. □ *No more! I'm completely podged!* □ *Eat till you're podged!*

poll students who obtain no more than a pass degree from Cambridge University. □ *Come on! You can do better than just be a poll!* □ *I suppose most students have to end up as polls.*

pong a stink or unpleasant smell. □ *Where is that terrible pong coming from?* □ *I just can't stand that pong.*

pongo 1. a soldier. □ *I'd never be a pongo if I could help it!* □ *Who's the pongo Mart's with tonight?* **2.** an orangutan. □ *Originally,*

131

pongos were thought to be sort of cavemen. □ *That's why a pongo is called an orangutan, which means "wild man" in Malay.* **3.** a foreigner. (Offensive.) □ *Otto did not like that pongo, and he made that clear to the poor guy in the strongest possible way.* □ *There seem to be a lot of pongos around here these days.* **4.** a monkey. □ *My uncle has a pet pongo.* □ *Pongos are supposed to eat peanuts and bananas.*

pony 1. to defecate. (Crude. Rhyming slang, linked as follows: pony [and trap] ≈ [crap] = defecate.) □ *Where do you go around here?* □ *He had to go to pony.* **2.** £25 (twenty-five pounds). (Compare with **gorilla** and **monkey**.) □ *All right, here's a pony. Don't spend it all in one shop.* □ *Can you lend me a pony till pay-day?*

poodle-faker a young man of effete or over-refined manners, who appears to cultivate the company of older ladies. (The implication is that he is faking the behaviour of a lapdog.) □ *Anthony looks like a real poodle-faker to me.* □ *I can't stand poodle-fakers like that.*

poof AND **poofter; pooftah; poove; pouffe; puff** a male homosexual. (Crude.) □ *So what if he's a poof? He can still vote, can't he?* □ *He doesn't like being called a pooftah.*

pooftah See poof.

poofter See poof.

poofy smelly. □ *What a poofy place this is!* □ *The trouble is that while he's poofy, his information is usually kosher.*

the **Pool** Liverpool. □ *The Beatles came from the Pool.* □ *The Pool is on the Mersey, in northwestern England.*

poor show not good enough; disappointing. □ *If it's a poor show, why do we continue to pretend it is not?* □ *Let's face it, this thing has turned out to be a pretty poor show.*

poove See poof.

pop it See pop one's clogs.

pop off See pop one's clogs.

pop one's clogs AND **pop it; pop off** to die. □ *My uncle popped his clogs last week.* □ *I hope I'm asleep when I pop it.*

pop-shop a pawn shop. □ *That place with the three balls above the door is a pop-shop, Victoria.* □ *Uncle's off to the pop-shop again.*

pop something to pawn something. □ *I've got nothing left to pop.* □ *I tried to pop my watch to get some money.*

porker a policeman. (Derived from pig.) □ *That porker will catch up with you some day.* □ *See that porker over there? He lifted me once.*

porky (pie) a lie. (Rhyming slang.) □ *That's not another of your porky pies, is it Johnny?* □ *A porky is only going to work if people believe it, you know.*

porridge time spent in jail. □ *Otto's been given a year's porridge.* □ *How much porridge did you get?*

post 1. mail collection. □ *Has the post been collected yet?* □ *No, you've ten minutes to the post.* **2.** mail delivery. □ *Has the post been delivered yet?* □ *No, here comes the post now.*

postie a postman or postwoman. □ *The postie usually is here before 8 a.m.* □ *We've had the same postie in this village for years.*

pot and pan a father or husband. (Rhyming slang, linked as follows: pot and pan ≈ [(old) man] = father.) □ *The boy's pot and pan is here looking for you.* □ *The pot and pan sat on the bench and waited for him.*

pouffe See poof.

prannet AND **pranny** a fool. □ *How can you be such a prannet?* □ *I felt like a pranny when I found out that I'd got onto the wrong train.*

pranny See prannet.

preggers pregnant. □ *Had you heard? Cynthia's preggers again.* □ *I can see she's preggers again.*

prezzie a present or gift. □ *What a lovely prezzie, darling. Thank you.* □ *This will make the perfect prezzie.*

price a chance. (From the habit of bookies of assigning starting prices only upon horses they believe have a significant chance of occupying one of the first three or four finishing positions in a race.) □ *There's a price here if you would just take it.* □ *He's just looking for the right price.*

private hire a car rented together with a driver. □ *It must be posh. They've arrived in a private hire.* □ *The private hire is here. Are you ready?*

professor a professional cricketer. □ *You know the rules—no professors on either team.* □ *I'm sorry, but we are strictly amateur and a professor would be against the club rules.*

prog a proctor at Oxford or Cambridge University. □ *The responsibility of the prog is to maintain discipline in the college.* □ *Who would be a prog in this day and age?*

pronk a fool. □ *That pronk thinks he can convince them.* □ *I felt like such a bloody pronk when I found out that I'd got onto the wrong train.*

proper 1. total or complete; quite (a). □ *This is a proper mess.* □ *That girl is becoming a proper little madam.* **2.** in a correct and polite way of speaking. □ *Please talk proper, Mary.* □ *They tell you to speak proper in there.*

proper charlie AND **right charlie** a complete fool; someone who looks foolish. □ *Who's the proper charlie in the bright orange trousers?* □ *Martin can be a right charlie at times.*

proper do a first-class party or other social event. □ *Fred knows how to put on a proper do!* □ *Now that really was a proper do!*

proverbial 1. the **proverbial** faeces. (A euphemism.) □ *Watch out, there's a pile of the proverbial over there, left by some dog.* □ *Get this sorted out or we'll all end up in the proverbial.* **2.** the **proverbials** the buttocks. (A euphemism.) □ *If that boy does not get a move on, give him a kick in the proverbials for me.* □ *I slipped on some ice and landed on my proverbials.*

prune a stupid person. (Offensive. Also a term of address.) □ *You prune! Why have you done that!* □ *Some prune forgot to get petrol today and his car has run dry.*

Pudding and Gravy See Lumpy Gravy.

puff See poof.

puff-adder an accountant. (Offensive. Derived as follows: puff-adder ≈ [addition] = [accounts] = accountant.) □ *The puff-adder says we've got to do something about our cash flow problem.* □ *When the puff-adders get finished with the numbers, you won't recognise them.*

puff and dart to start or commence. (Rhyming slang.) □ *Time to puff and dart, eh?* □ *We puffed and darted, and it was not so bad as I thought.*

pukka 1. authentic. (From Hindi, meaning "well cooked" or "substantial.") □ *I'm afraid his pukka Porsche turns out to be a ringer.* □ *Of course it's pukka fake gold leaf.* **2.** reliable. □ *Harry said to make sure we've only got pukka people on the team.* □ *This is a pukka piece of machinery. When you need it, it will work.* **3.** of full measure. □ *Oh no, this is the full, pukka version.* □ *But I ordered the pukka one!*

pull about 1. to treat someone roughly. □ *The thugs pulled me about a bit but I'm all right.* □ *Come on, you don't have to pull him about like that.* **2.** to knock from side to side. □ *The little yacht was pulled about in the storm, and I worried if we were going to make it.* □ *The vibrations really pulled about the aircraft for a while.*

pull a flanker (on someone) See *do a flanker (on someone)*.

pull a stroke 1. to commit a successful crime. □ *Mr Big can work out how to pull a stroke.* □ *Otto actually pulls the strokes that Mr Big plans.* **2.** to successfully carry out a deception or trick. □ *I think we can pull a stroke here.* □ *Why do you keep pulling these cruel strokes on me?*

pull the moody to sulk. □ *I'm not pulling the moody, Lavinia.* □ *Oh, why must you always pull the moody on me, Albert?*

punch-up a fistfight. □ *Stop that punch-up now.* □ *I will not tolerate punch-ups around here.*

pure dead brilliant wonderful; marvellous. (Scots usage.) □ *What a pure dead brilliant idea!* □ *Ah think that singer's pure dead brilliant, so Ah do!*

purler a blow that causes the victim to fall head first. □ *He delivered a violent purler, and Joe fell.* □ *Did you see how he fell? That was some purler!*

push-start to start a car by pushing it along in order to turn over the engine and get it firing. □ *The middle of the night in the middle of nowhere and I'm out in the rain push-starting your car. Oh yes, I'm impressed I must say.* □ *If all else fails we'll just have to push-start it.*

push the boat out to celebrate in a big way. □ *We're planning on pushing the boat out again tonight.* □ *We pushed the boat out till 4 a.m.*

put about to spread a rumour. □ *What's this story you're putting about about me?* □ *If you put about lies, people will get very angry indeed.*

put a spoke in someone's wheel(s) to prevent or delay someone's intended action. □ *I wish they would not continually try to put a spoke in our wheels.* □ *The time to put a spoke in her wheel has come, I think.*

put someone in the pudding club to make someone pregnant. (Crude.) □ *I don't think he intended to put her in the pudding club, you know.* □ *I put her in the pudding club, and now the baby's due next month.*

put someone on the mat to reprimand someone severely. □ *I must really put you on the mat this morning.* □ *I'm afraid that after that little exhibition, we will have to put you on the mat.*

put the black on someone to threaten to blackmail someone. □ *Otto threatened to put the black on him.* □ *I don't want anyone to put the black on me.*

put the boot in AND **sink the boot in 1.** to attack unnecessarily after victory is certain. □ *Otto certainly knows how to put the boot in.* □ *He did not hesitate to sink the boot in.* **2.** to kick an opponent who is already on the floor. □ *He was down, but still they put the boot in.* □ *To sink the boot in after the guy is downed is considered rather wicked.*

put the frighteners on someone to scare or frighten someone. □ *Otto's been putting the frighteners on the witnesses for the prosecution.* □ *Don't you try to put the frighteners on me, sunshine!*

put the mockers on someone 1. to curse someone. □ *I think she's put the mockers on me.* □ *He threatened to put the mockers on her.* **2.** to ruin or stop someone. □ *Some fool put the mockers on us today.* □ *Don't try to put the mockers on me son, if you know what's good for you.*

putty medal a trivial or humorous reward for a small service. □ *He got a putty medal for that, would you believe.* □ *I didn't think there was enough even for a putty medal.*

put up the shutters to go out of business; to quit. □ *They put up the shutters last week.* □ *We'll all be putting up the shutters soon if the economy doesn't pick up.*

quaggy shaky or difficult. □ *Calculus is too quaggy for me.* □ *This arrangement is still very quaggy.*

Quaker Oat(s) a coat. (Rhyming slang.) □ *That's a ridiculous Quaker Oats. I won't wear it.* □ *I've lost my Quaker Oat.*

the **Qualities** the better-class newspapers (as a group) as opposed to the down-market tabloids. □ *All the Qualities are saying the government will fall this week.* □ *What do the Qualities have to say about the situation in South America?*

quarter-bloke a quartermaster. □ *Go and see the quarter-bloke about that, soldier.* □ *The squaddies are at the quarter-bloke, getting fitted out for uniforms.*

Queen Anne is dead. That's very old news. □ *Yes, we won World War II, and Queen Anne is dead, too.* □ *Where have you been all this time? Queen Anne is dead.*

Queer Street AND **Slump Alley** Carey Street in London. (See also in Queer Street.) □ *That's Queer Street, where the Bankruptcy Court is to be found.* □ *It's Slump Alley for you, my lad.*

queer the pitch to secretly spoil or ruin an opportunity. □ *Don't queer the pitch for me son, if you know what's good for you.* □ *Some fool queered our pitch today.*

queue-barge See queue jump.

queue jump AND **jump the queue; queue-barge** to move in front of those waiting in a queue. □ *Walter is an expert at queue jumping.* □ *Anyone who queue-barges goes to the rear to start again. OK?*

quid one pound sterling. (The plural is the same.) □ *Have you got a few quid you can spare?* □ *These things cost more than just a few quid.*

quids in **1.** going well. □ *Well, things are quids in now, I must say.* □ *How are things? Quids in of course!* **2.** making a profit. □ *Now we're quids in!* □ *Exert yourself and you'll be quids in with ease.*

quod prison. □ *Otto's in quod, and will be there for some time I think.* □ *Have you ever been in the quod?*

R

rabbit inconsequential chatter. (Rhyming slang, linked as follows: rabbit [and pork] ≈ [talk] = chatter. Compare with bunny.) □ *There's never anything but rabbit between these two.* □ *Why do you always have to make such trivial rabbit all the time?*

rabbit something to borrow but fail to return something. □ *What does she want to rabbit this time?* □ *That's not fair. She does not mean to rabbit things. It's just that she forgets to bring them back.*

the rads the police. □ *The rads broke up the fight.* □ *The rads finally caught up with Gert.*

the Raff the Royal Air Force. (A near-acronym from *RAF*.) □ *Brian was a pilot in the Raff for a number of years.* □ *There's a Raff base near here.*

rag order a chaotic mess. □ *How did you create such a rag order here?* □ *What a rag order you've made of this!*

rain stair-rods to rain very heavily. □ *It was really raining stair-rods so we went to the pictures.* □ *I hate driving when it's raining stair-rods like that.*

raise the wind to raise money required for a particular purpose. □ *I'm still trying to raise the wind for the development.* □ *How much wind do you still have to raise?*

ramp 1. to swindle. □ *Watch it, he's trying to ramp you.* □ *I think they are trying to ramp us in some way or other.* **2.** a swindle. □ *This is an okay ramp you've got going here.* □ *They pulled a real dirty ramp on that old lady.* **3.** the counter of the bar in a public house. □ *All the regulars have their own places along the ramp in here.* □ *He pushed his way through the crowd to the ramp in order to place an order with the barman.*

ram-raid a smash-and-grab robbery where access is made into a store by ramming into its front with a vehicle. □ *The gang chose*

139

the electrical store for their next ram-raid. □ Right, you go and nick a Range Rover for the ram-raid.

Raquel Welch a belch. (Rhyming slang.) □ She released a discrete Raquel Welch behind her hanky, thinking no one would notice. □ Try not to do a Raquel Welch at table, Johnny.

ratbag a disgusting or very unpleasant person. (Offensive. Also a term of address.) □ What a ratbag that woman can be. □ Get out of here, you ratbag!

rate of knots a high speed. □ The Concorde really does move at a rate of knots. □ If you really want to drive at a rate of knots, try the German autobahnen where there is no speed limit.

rattle and clank a bank. (Rhyming slang. This refers to the sort of bank where money is kept.) □ When does that rattle and clank open today, please? □ That's the rattle and clank where I keep my money.

rattler a bicycle. □ How much did that rattler set you back? □ You have to wear a helmet with a rattler that size, don't you?

rattling good excellent. □ Her party was really rattling good. □ What a rattling good place to live!

raver a dedicated party-goer. □ Now Sally is your right little raver, all right! □ There go these ravers at last. What time of night do they think this is?

razor-edge 1. a very sharp edge. □ Watch out! That's a real razor-edge there. □ I had not realised the corner was such a razor-edge. **2.** a critical situation. □ We've got a bit of a razor-edge here, so take care. □ When it's razor-edge like this, it's very difficult. **3.** a mountain ridge which forms a distinct dividing line. □ If you look over there to the mountains, you can see the razor-edge quite clearly. □ We actually stood on the razor-edge for a while and took in the spectacular views of both valleys. **4.** a boundary line marking a sharp division. □ Here's the razor-edge. Don't even think of crossing it! □ The division between the two areas of the factory was quite obvious. Everyone could see the razor-edge.

razor-edged [of a disagreement] sharp. □ Oh, not another razor-edged argument like last night! □ The disagreement has been razor-edged for weeks now.

reach-me-down 1. [of clothes] inherited; hand-me-down. □ I'm not going to wear reach-me-downs! □ I'd wear reach-me-downs, *but not ones that look like reach-me-downs.* **2.** [of clothes] ready-made. □ *Only poor people wear reach-me-down clothes, Mum!* □ *We came across this shop selling nothing but reach-me-down dresses.*

read and write to fight. (Rhyming slang.) □ *The read and write was a bit of a failure as the other side failed to show!* □ *Well, if that's really how you feel, let's arrange another read and write!*

readies cash or ready money. □ *Sorry, I can't afford it, I've no readies.* □ *How much readies do you need, then?*

real chuffed See dead chuffed.

the **real Mackay** AND the **real McCoy** something authentic. □ *This is the real Mackay. Nothing else like it.* □ *This is no copy. It's the real McCoy.*

real McCoy See real Mackay.

red, white, and blue a shoe. (Rhyming slang.) □ *I find these red, white, and blues uncomfortable.* □ *Why are you in these red, white, and blues? Are you going somewhere?*

reeb beer. (Backslang.) □ *Can I have reeb, please?* □ *I do like this reeb they have in here.*

Reverend (Ronald Knox) venereal disease. (Crude. Rhyming slang, linked as follows: Reverend (Ronald Knox) ≈ [pox] = venereal disease.) □ *A visit from the Reverend Ronald Knox is not really funny, you know.* □ *All right, it's true, I've got the Reverend.*

rhino money. □ *I don't make enough rhino to go on a trip like that!* □ *It takes a lot of rhino to buy a car like that.*

rhubarb (pill) a bill. (Rhyming slang. This refers to the sort of bill that has to be paid.) □ *How much did the rhubarb pill come to?* □ *No, no, it's my rhubarb. I insist on paying.*

right as ninepence in perfect condition. □ *I'm fine, as right as ninepence!* □ *If you're as right as ninepence, why are you here?*

right charlie See proper charlie.

right-ho a term of agreement. □ *Right-ho, I'll go right away.* □ *Right-ho! I'm very pleased with that.*

right one a foolish person. □ *Well! We've got a right one here!* □ *You're not going to make a right one out of me.*

right shut completely shut. □ *Make sure that door's right shut!* □ *The door was not right shut and a cold draught blew into the house.*

right up one's street AND **up one's street** exactly one's kind of thing; exactly what one is best equipped to do. □ *That job is right up her street.* □ *It's not exactly up my street, but I'll try it.*

rigout a set of clothes. □ *I feel sort of funny in this rigout.* □ *Where did you get a rigout like that to wear?*

ring back to return a telephone call. □ *You better ring back. It seemed important.* □ *Hello, I'm just ringing back.*

ring through See phone through.

ring up See phone through.

rinky-dink neat; pretty. □ *Yes, it is rinky-dink.* □ *That is a pretty rinky-dink car you have there.*

River Ouse an alcoholic drink. (Rhyming slang, linked as follows: River Ouse ≈ [booze] = alcoholic drink. The Ouse is a river that flows into the Wash on the eastern coast of England.) □ *Now that's what I'd call River Ouse.* □ *Any more of that River Ouse?*

rocket(ing) a strong reprimand. □ *You're just asking for a rocketing.* □ *What was that rocket for?*

rock of ages wages. (Rhyming slang.) □ *Have you collected this week's rock of ages from the pay office yet?* □ *So when I got my rock of ages there was far more deducted than I'd expected.*

rod in pickle trouble in store. □ *I'm sure you're going to find the rod in pickle for you, sunshine.* □ *I know I've got a rod in pickle waiting when I get home.*

Roller a Rolls-Royce car. □ *Like my new Roller, darling?* □ *I'm rather partial to Rollers.*

rollock to chastise someone severely. □ *Did the lad really deserve being rollocked like that?* □ *Mr Big really knows how to rollock someone.*

rollocking See bollocking.

roly-poly pudding a dessert consisting of a strip or sheet of suet pastry covered with jam or fruit, then rolled and baked or steamed. □ *Bill loves his mother's roly-poly pudding.* □ *Please can I have more roly-poly pudding, mum?*

ronk 1. to stink. □ *When we opened the room it ronked very badly.* □ *If you've got to ronk like a badger's backside, do so a long way from me.* **2.** a stink. □ *I just can't stand that ronk.* □ *Where is that terrible ronk coming from?*

rop(e)y 1. low-grade or substandard. □ *The stuff in today's delivery was very ropey so we sent it back.* □ *Sorry, these products are too ropy for us.* **2.** somewhat unwell. □ *Oh dear, I feel really ropey.* □ *Carol is a bit ropy today, I'm afraid.* **3.** unreliable; untrustworthy. □ *He's got a ropey heart, you know.* □ *I'm afraid this car of mine's a bit ropy.* **4.** smelly; unpleasant. □ *The trouble is that although he's ropey, his information is usually kosher.* □ *A strange ropy ambience pervaded the whole area.*

rorty 1. enjoyable; boisterous. □ *The men always used to have a great rorty time after the harvest was all in.* □ *The party became a bit loud and rorty later on.* **2.** fond of amusement. □ *Oh, old Bert is rorty all right. What sort of entertainment are you thinking of?* □ *There were several rorty busloads in the theatre that night.* **3.** unsophisticated or crude. □ *She's a bit like that. Anything in the least rorty is disapproved of.* □ *I think this pub may be a bit too rorty for me.* **4.** down to earth. □ *All right, let's keep this discussion rorty.* □ *To be completely rorty, what I really want is money. Lots of money.*

Rosie Lee a flea. (Rhyming slang.) □ *Is that . . . no, it couldn't be . . . a Rosie Lee on your coat?* □ *There were Rosie Lees everywhere throughout the old house.*

Rosie Loader a whisky and soda. (Rhyming slang.) □ *The Rosie Loaders were certainly flowing that evening, I can tell you.* □ *I could use a Rosie Loader.*

rot 1. nonsense. □ *Don't give me any more of your rot. Speak straight or shut up.* □ *What utter rot! Don't believe any of it!* **2.** to joke. □ *Those people just rot around all day.* □ *Stop rotting and start working.* **3.** to tease or annoy. □ *Stop rotting him, Johnny.* □ *Why do children always rot each other?*

rotter an objectionable person. (Offensive. Also a term of address.) □ *What a rotter you are!* □ *Just get out of my sight, you rotter!*

rouf AND **ruof** four. (Criminal backslang. See also **French loaf**.) □ Q: *How much did you get?* A: *Just a measly rouf quid, mate.* □ *I could use ruof right now. I'm broke.*

rough unwell. □ *Oh dear, I feel rather rough.* □ *Carol is a bit rough today, I'm afraid.*

rough diamond someone who is wonderful despite a rough exterior; someone with great potential that has yet to develop.

□ *Although Sam looks a little tacky, really he's a rough diamond.*
□ *He's a rough diamond—a little hard to take at times, but okay mostly.*

rough tongue rude or harsh language. □ *What a rough tongue that man has!* □ *She felt the strength of my rough tongue, I fear.*

round the houses trousers. (Rhyming slang. This is a rather poor rhyme that has to be worked at a bit.) □ *Why are you wearing bright green round the houses?* □ *These round the houses look ridiculous on you.*

Royal Mail See holy nail.

rozzer a policeman. □ *Think about how the rozzer on the beat is affected by this cold.* □ *The rozzer stopped at the door, tried the lock, and moved on.*

rub-a-dub-dub a pub. (Rhyming slang.) □ *That's not a bad little rub-a-dub-dub you've got there, mate.* □ *He's down the rub-a-dub-dub, as usual.*

rubber cheque a cheque that is worthless. (Because, like rubber, it bounces.) □ *The bank says I wrote a rubber cheque, but I'm sure there was enough money in my account.* □ *One rubber cheque after another! Can't you add?*

rubbish 1. to criticise someone with exceptional severity. □ *I'm tired of listening to you rubbishing every idea I come out with.* □ *Your ideas are rubbished because they are rubbish!* □ *I do wish you would not rubbish people like that.* **2.** to discard something as useless. □ *Why do you have to rubbish everything?* □ *I'm afraid I'm going to have to rubbish that plan, too.*

ruby red the head. (Rhyming slang.) □ *Put your hat on your ruby red, and let's go.* □ *That's using your ruby red!*

ruck 1. a heated argument. □ *Who started this ruck anyway?* □ *I'm sorry about that ruck we had yesterday, but it was all your fault.* **2.** a fight between gangs. □ *That was some ruck last night.* □ *Who's going to win the ruck, I ask?*

rucker a gang fighter. □ *I'd be nice to him, he's a rucker.* □ *Why are we trying to talk to ruckers?*

rucking a severe criticism. □ *You are going to get a terrible rucking after that remark.* □ *Did they really deserve a rucking like that?*

ruddy bloody. (Crude. A euphemism or disguise.) □ *Why should I stop ruddy swearing just 'cos you ruddy tell me?* □ *Who the ruddy hell do you ruddy well think you are?*

rudery a rude remark. □ *Now there was some rudery that was not called for, I think.* □ *Try to cut out the rudery when speaking to clients, Otto.*

rumble to discover something that had been deliberately hidden. □ *I think I've rumbled what you're up to!* □ *They've rumbled it.*

ruof See rouf.

rush one's fences to attempt to move or work too fast. □ *Please don't rush your fences. We may be wrong.* □ *If you rush your fences, you may miss something important.*

S

the **Sally** AND the **Sally Army**; the **Sally-Ann** the Salvation Army.
□ *Mary plays a tambourine in the Sally band.* □ *The Sally-Ann have a hostel for homeless people along this street.*

the **Sally-Ann** See Sally.

the **Sally Army** See Sally.

salmon and trout stout beer. (Rhyming slang.) □ *How about a salmon and trout before you go, Charlie?* □ *Give my friend here a salmon and trout.*

sarky See narky.

sarnie a sandwich. □ *Fancy a bacon and tomato sarnie?* □ *Once we had to live on sarnies, being too poor for anything fancier.*

saucepan lid a one pound note or coin. (Rhyming slang, linked as follows: saucepan lid ≈ [quid] = pound note. The pound note has now been replaced by the one pound coin, except in Scotland.) □ *Is that all you can manage? One miserable saucepan lid?* □ *I handed him a saucepan lid and he looked back at me, smiling.*

sausage a goose to cash a cheque. □ *Where can I sausage a goose round here, mate?* □ *Harry'll sausage a goose, I think.*

sausage and mash 1. cash. (Rhyming slang.) □ *I don't have any sausage and mash.* □ *What do you want sausage and mash for, anyway?* **2.** a crash. (Rhyming slang.) □ *There's been a bad sausage and mash at the road intersection.* □ *What caused the sausage and mash to your computer this time?*

scarper to escape, flee, or run away. □ *There was no time to scarper, so we had to talk to Mrs Wilson.* □ *Lefty tried to scarper.*

scatty scatterbrained. □ *Who is that scatty girl in the red dress?* □ *That sweet little old lady is completely scatty, you do realise.*

scoff food. □ *This scoff is grim!* □ *I want some good old British scoff.*

scoff (up) something to eat something voraciously. □ *He's scoffing up all the food he can find.* □ *She scoffed three hamburgers and a large portion of chips.*

scone the head. □ *Turn your scone around and take a look at this.* □ *He's distinctive because he has a particularly large scone.*

scoobs beer. (Military slang derived from the children's TV show *Scooby Doo, Where Are You?* The usage dates from the 1991 Gulf War in Saudi Arabia, land of no alcohol.) □ *Have a can of scoobs, Charlie.* □ *Here, that's good scoobs!*

scoop the pool 1. to make a financial killing. □ *She's dreamt of scooping the pool for decades.* □ *So, how do we scoop the pool?* **2.** to win a bet in a big way. □ *Yippee! I've scooped the pool!* □ *If you scoop the pool again, a lot of people will not speak to you.*

Scotch mist intoxicated due to drink. (Crude. Rhyming slang, linked as follows: Scotch mist ≈ [pissed] = intoxicated.) □ *They were both very Scotch mist. They could only lie there and snore.* □ *Tracy gets quite Scotch mist after just a drink or two.*

Scouse the dialect spoken in Liverpool. (Offensive.) □ *Scouse is a dialect unique to Liverpool.* □ *He was speaking Scouse, I think. I understood nothing.*

Scouser a native or inhabitant of Liverpool. □ *All the Beatles were Scousers.* □ *I can't understand a Scouser speaking in dialect.*

scran military rations. □ *Is that all we've got here? Scran?* □ *I once lived on nothing but scran for over a week.*

scroat AND **scrote** a despicable person. □ *Get out of here, you scroat!* □ *What a scrote that woman can be.*

scrote See scroat.

scruff a scruffy or untidy person. □ *Her boyfriend is a little scruff, but he's a rich little scruff!* □ *He says scruffs like us don't dress well enough for his restaurant!*

scrummage 1. a frenetic crowd. □ *That's a huge scrummage there tonight, she thought.* □ *They were all struggling to get through the scrummage coming out of the football match.* **2.** a place of confusion. □ *The place was just a huge scrummage.* □ *I'm not going to go to a scrummage like that again.*

scrummy AND **yummy** delicious; delightful. □ *What a scrummy cake!* □ *She said she had a yummy idea for the weekend.*

scrump to steal fruit from an orchard. □ *I was only scrumping, officer!* □ *It's still a crime to scrump, son.*

scuffer a policeman. □ *The scuffer stopped at the door, tried the lock, and moved on.* □ *Think about how the scuffer on the beat is affected by this cold.*

see over something to inspect something, a house for example. □ *We went to see over that house we're thinking of buying.* □ *Can I see over this car you have for sale?*

sell a pup to swindle by selling that which is worthless. □ *That lot sold you a pup. They must have seen you coming.* □ *Hey! Give me my money back! I've been sold a pup!*

send someone down 1. to expel from a university. □ *He's been sent down for theft.* □ *Not so many people get sent down from university nowadays.* **2.** to sentence someone to a term of imprisonment. □ *I am sending you down for a period of two years.* □ *I got sent down for assault.*

send someone to Coventry to ostracise someone. □ *After what he did, it was hardly surprising they sent him to Coventry.* □ *It's not often that the men send someone to Coventry.*

septic 1. offensive; disagreeable. (A jocular derivative from *sceptic*.) □ *I'm afraid he really is a septic little person.* □ *That was a septic thing to do.* **2. Septic** See Septic Tank.

Septic (Tank) an American. (Rhyming slang, linked as follows: Septic (Tank) ≈ [Yank] = American.) □ *Mr Big's talking to a Septic Tank just now.* □ *Some Septic was here looking for you this afternoon.*

set the Thames on fire to make a great success in life, etc. □ *Well, you've not exactly set the Thames on fire so far, have you?* □ *I don't want to set the Thames on fire, but just to live quietly.*

Seven Dials haemorrhoids. (Rhyming slang, linked as follows: Seven Dials ≈ [piles] = haemorrhoids. Seven Dials is a district in London.) □ *A bad dose of the Seven Dials is sheer hell.* □ *Our Bert suffers terribly from the Seven Dials, you know.*

shackles a thick soup made from leftovers. □ *Fancy a bowl of shackles?* □ *There's nothing better than some shackles on a cold day.*

shamrock tea very weak tea. (Figuratively, tea with just three leaves in it.) □ *Now this was real shamrock tea, barely distinguishable from hot water.* □ *I can't stand shamrock tea!*

sharpish 1. quite rapidly. □ *Move sharpish!* □ *Get a sharpish move on, you lot.* **2.** quite sharp. □ *Oh yes, he's sharpish all right.* □ *That's a sharpish knife you have there.*

shed a tear to urinate. (Crude.) □ *Well, shedding a tear does relieve the pressure of all that beer!* □ *I'm just going to shed a tear.*

sheet a banknote. □ *Sorry, I don't have any sheets with me. Can you pay?* □ *He put a number of sheets into the top pocket of my shirt and said that there was plenty more to be had if I asked no questions.*

shekels pounds sterling; money. □ *Have you got a few shekels you can spare?* □ *These things cost plenty of shekels.*

shell-like an ear. □ *Allow me to take you to one side and have a word in your shell-like, sonny.* □ *Look at the huge shell-likes on her!*

sherbet liquor or beer. □ *I could use a little sherbet with this soft stuff.* □ *Larry hid all his sherbet under the bed.*

shin off to go away. □ *You know, I told him to shin off and he did!* □ *Look, why don't you just shin off?*

shoot the lights to cross a junction when the red "stop" light is showing. □ *He shot the lights and was booked.* □ *Don't try shooting the lights. It's not worth it.*

shop to inform against someone, especially to the police. □ *Who shopped me?* □ *I didn't shop you!*

shop-window any opportunity to exhibit products, talents, etc. □ *You've got a great shop-window there. Use it!* □ *I'd like a shop-window for my talents.*

shout the purchase of a round of drinks. □ *Come on! It's your shout!* □ *All right, all right, it's my shout. What do you want to drink this time?*

shout and holler a collar. (Rhyming slang.) □ *He hates wearing a shout and holler.* □ *You've got to have on a shout and holler to get in there.*

shove(l) along to move along without fuss. □ *Shovel along, please.* □ *They shoved along, making room for the others.*

shovel and broom a room. (Rhyming slang.) □ *This is my shovel and broom. Sod off!* □ *I got back to me shovel and broom and shut the door.*

shovel and tank a bank. (Rhyming slang. This refers to the kind of bank where money is kept.) □ *That's the shovel and tank where I keep my money.* □ *When does that shovel and tank open today, please?*

shower an objectionable or unacceptable person or group of people. □ *The same shower was waiting outside the office for him as he left.* □ *They're just a shower.*

shreddies torn, tattered, or otherwise disgusting underwear. □ *How could anyone wear shreddies like that?* □ *First, let's get you out of these terrible shreddies.*

shufti AND **shufty** a glimpse or quick glance. □ *He took a shufti but saw nothing unusual.* □ *Take a shufty at that!*

shufty See shufti.

shunt a traffic accident involving two or more vehicles. □ *There was a bad shunt outside the office this morning.* □ *Several people were injured in the shunt.*

sick vomit. □ *Mummy, there's sick all over the carpet.* □ *I think it's cat sick, Jimmy.*

sideboards side-whiskers or sideburns. □ *I don't trust men with sideboards.* □ *He's the fellow with the great big sideboards.*

sidley stylishly furtive; hypocritically arrogant. □ *If you were less sidley, you'd get more done.* □ *Why do you always have to be so sidley?*

sidy affected with pomposity or boastfulness. □ *What a sidy character he is!* □ *Why does he always have to be so sidy?*

silver plate please. (From the French *s'il vous plaît*, which means this, by hobson-jobson.) □ *Can I have my purse back? Silver plate?* □ *Silver plate! I need an answer!*

Singers Singapore. □ *I'm off to Singers on business next week.* □ *Meet Simon, just back from Singers.*

single a single, or one-way, travel ticket. □ *A single to Manchester, please.* □ *How much is a single from here to London?*

sink the boot in See put the boot in.

six months hard a card. (Rhyming slang.) □ *He turned over the six months hard saying, "My game, I think!"* □ *Holding out the fanned-out pack, he asked Otto to pick a six months hard.*

skating rink a bald head. □ *You'll recognise him because of his skating rink.* □ *I like men with skating rinks.*

skew-whiff out of alignment. □ *You've hung this door skew-whiff.* □ *I'm afraid a skew-whiff machine like that is quite useless.*

skin and blister a sister. (Rhyming slang.) □ *Terry's here, and he's brought his skin and blister with him.* □ *Can I bring me skin and blister?*

skit a large crowd. □ *It was strange that there was such a skit, today of all days.* □ *The skit was pressing in towards the stadium.*

skive 1. a ploy or ruse to shirk duty or responsibility. □ *Yes, it's a cunning skive, but I don't think it'll work.* □ *Who thought up that skive, Otto?* **2.** See **skive off**.

skive (off) to evade or shirk duty or responsibility. □ *Hoy! Where do you think you're skiving off to?* □ *No more skiving. There's work to be done here.*

skiver someone who avoids duty or responsibility. □ *I don't want that skiver on my team.* □ *If you want to be a skiver, go and be one somewhere else.*

skivvy a female drudge or servant. □ *Why does everybody treat me like a skivvy?* □ *Because you are a skivvy, that's why.*

skull a passenger. □ *Fourteen skulls and crew of fifteen? I don't think this is a profitable route for a 747.* □ *Driving buses would be great fun if we didn't have to carry skulls.*

slagging a severe criticism. □ *Did they really deserve a slagging like that?* □ *You are going to get a terrible slagging after that remark.*

slaggy low, in the pejorative sense. □ *Why, you slaggy little tyke!* □ *I don't want anything to do with that sort of slaggy deal.*

slap-up [of a meal] first-rate or lavish; extravagant. □ *They're planning a really slap-up do for Donna's retirement.* □ *Well, that was a slap-up meal!*

slate someone off to disparage someone. □ *Don't just slate him off! He's right!* □ *To slate off people all the time is not a good way to be popular with the folks closest to you.*

slinky 1. sneaky; sly; furtive. □ *That was very slinky. How did you do it?* □ *Well, you're a slinky one!* **2.** smooth; sensuous; clinging. □ *What a lovely slinky dress you are wearing this evening, Mary.* □ *Just feel the slinky texture of this material.*

slip in the gutter bread and butter. (Rhyming slang, linked as follows: slip in the gutter ≈ [butter] = bread and butter.) □ *She gave me a few slices of slip in the gutter.* □ *I'd rather like some slip in the gutter.*

slog an extended spell of hard work. □ *Look, I know it's a slog, but it just has to be done.* □ *Once the slog is over, you'll enjoy things here more.*

slop AND **esclop** the police. (Backslang.) □ *Get away, get away! The slop are outside!* □ *The esclop are after me!*

sloughed dead. (A hospital euphemism.) □ *Another sloughed one just came in.* □ *That's three sloughed customers already tonight.*

slubber to stain or spoil something. □ *Don't you dare slubber my best tablecloth!* □ *Oh no! Someone has slubbered all over these things.*

Slump Alley See Queer Street.

slush counterfeit banknotes. □ *The police have been warning of a rash of slush in this area, so watch out.* □ *She held the note up to the light and said, "If you want to pass slush you'll have to make better forgeries than that!"*

slusher a counterfeiter. □ *Out there, some slusher is making a lot of very good fake coins.* □ *The police picked up a slusher tonight.*

slushy cloyingly sentimental. □ *Harry always laughs at slushy rubbish in a film.* □ *The love scenes were real out-and-out slushy, but nobody laughed.*

smack on See bang on.

the **Smoke** See Big Smoke.

smudger a friend. □ *This is my smudger, Wally.* □ *We've been smudgers for years. Went to school together.*

snake bite a drink consisting of cider and lager in equal portions. □ *You know how snake bite disagrees with you, my dear.* □ *I often enjoy a snake bite in the evening.*

snide 1. unacceptable; inferior in quality. □ *Sorry, it's too snide for me.* □ *That sort of behaviour is just snide, you know.* **2.** counterfeit; dishonest; illegal; stolen. □ *All right Harry, where did this snide stuff come from?* □ *We found a huge stock of snide coins.*

snog 1. to kiss and caress in an amorous way. □ *Let's go somewhere quiet and snog.* □ *There are some teenagers in the back room,* *snogging.* **2.** to flirt. □ *Those two have been snogging like that for months.* □ *She only wants to snog with me.*

snooker to prevent a continuation; to thwart. (From the game of snooker, where the purpose is to do this to one's opponent.) □ *It seems my entire career has been snookered.* □ *Why are you trying to snooker this development?*

snouter a tobacconist's shop. □ *My aunt used to have a snouter, but it's closed now.* □ *Is there a snouter around here?*

snuffer a veterinary surgeon. □ *Is there a decent snuffer for my dog in this town?* □ *We need a snuffer now. This is a really sick cat.*

sob one pound sterling. □ *These things cost more than just a few sobs.* □ *Have you got a sob you can spare?*

sob story a hard-luck story. □ *I've heard nothing but sob stories today. Isn't anybody happy?* □ *She had quite a sob story, and I listened to the whole thing.*

socked out out of commission; not functioning. □ *That machine is socked out, I'm afraid.* □ *Harry got the socked out unit working again.*

sod 1. a worthless or despised person, usually male. (Crude.) □ *Why do we employ that useless sod?* □ *The sod has just written off another company car.* **2.** an average or typical man. □ *The poor sod sat on the bench, just waiting.* □ *What is that sod here for, anyway?*

soft option the easiest or most comfortable of a number of choices available. □ *Trust you to choose the soft option every time!* □ *So, which one's the soft option, eh?*

soggies breakfast cereals. □ *Where are my usual soggies?* □ *I like my soggies at breakfast.*

something to be going on with See enough to be going on with.

song of the thrush a brush. (Rhyming slang.) □ *He took out a large song of the thrush and swept the driveway clear of leaves.* □ *Look at that delicate song of the thrush her Ladyship uses on her hair.*

sorry and sad bad. (Rhyming slang.) □ *This entire government is sorry and sad.* □ *That sorry and sad creep is asking for you again.*

sorted satisfactory; contented. □ *Don't worry, it's all sorted again now.* □ *It's fine. It's all sorted.*

Soup and Gravy See Lumpy Gravy.

souper a traitor; a defector. (Irish usage.) □ *If Mick weren't such a souper, I could stand him.* □ *You slimy little souper! How could you?*

spag bol AND **spaggers** spaghetti Bolognese; a way of serving spaghetti with chopped beef, onion, and tomato. (Originally from the city of Bologna in Italy.) □ *Fancy some spag bol for lunch?* □ *Spaggers is always a popular eating choice.*

spaggers See spag bol.

Spanish custom a shady or illegal practice. □ *Mike and Jack have a few handy Spanish customs working for them among the local street traders that bring them in a nice steady income.* □ *Well, Spanish customs are all very fine, so long as the rozzers don't get to hear about them!*

spanner in the works a problem or delay. □ *I'm afraid there is one spanner in the works.* □ *I don't want to hear about more spanners in the works.*

spare 1. idle; at a loose end. □ *Just looking at him you could see he was spare.* □ *Try not to look so spare all the time.* **2.** livid with rage. □ *So she went spare. Why should that affect you so much?* □ *I just knew you'd go spare.* **3.** crazy; insane. □ *Any more of this and I'll go spare.* □ *I'm spare with worry.*

sparkers unconscious; deeply asleep. □ *Who is that sparkers gal by the window?* □ *I'm still more than a bit sparkers. Give me a minute or two to wake up.*

sparkler 1. an electric train. □ *There are sparklers passing here all the time.* □ *Get the sparkler—that's the easy way to get there from here.* **2.** a helpful lie. □ *A lie is only a sparkler if people believe it, you know.* □ *That's not another of your sparklers, is it Johnny?*

spark out 1. to fall into a deep sleep. □ *He sparked out in seconds.* □ *I'm just going to spark out, all right?* **2.** to become unconscious through drink or drugs. □ *He sparked out halfway through the session.* □ *I don't know what was in that stuff but we all sparked out in no time.* **3.** to die. □ *For a minute, I thought I was going to spark out, too.* □ *He sparked out when his plane crashed during a training flight.*

speedo a speedometer. □ *He tapped the speedo again. "Nope!" he said. "It's broken."* □ *According to the speedo he was exceeding the speed limit by forty miles per hour. Could that have anything to do with the police car on his tail with siren blaring and lights flashing?*

spend a penny to go to the toilet. (Crude. A euphemism. From the former necessity to put a penny into the lock in order to gain access to a stall in a public toilet.) □ *Timmy has to spend a penny.* □ *Just a moment while I spend a penny.*

split new brand new. □ *How did Otto ever get hold of a split new BMW?* □ *How does Otto get a split new anything, do you think?*

split pea tea. (Rhyming slang.) □ *I could go some split pea.* □ *Where do you get a cup of split pea around here?*

spot of bother some slight trouble. □ *It looks as if there's a spot of bother ahead.* □ *Sorry for that spot of bother, folks.*

spot on exact or perfect. □ *Don't move! That's spot on!* □ *No, try to get it spot on this time.*

sprat to catch a mackerel a small risk that promises a large reward. □ *It's worth a sprat to catch a mackerel this time, I think.* □ *For such a large mackerel, it's well worth risking such a tiny sprat.*

sprauncy well presented, flashy, or showy. □ *Look at her! Have you ever seen anyone looking as sprauncy?* □ *If you did not dress so sprauncy you would not attract so many comments from passers-by.*

spruce to evade work or responsibility. □ *Mike's on the spruce again.* □ *Mike goes to great lengths to spruce, of course.*

spruce someone to deceive or confuse someone. □ *Don't spruce me! What happened?* □ *If you're going to spruce someone, don't get caught.*

squaddie 1. a private soldier. □ *Who's the squaddie Mart's with tonight?* □ *I'd never be a squaddie if I could help it!* **2.** a new recruit to the army. □ *Tom has just become a squaddie.* □ *He may just be a squaddie but he already looks a soldier.*

square-eyed concerning a reputed effect of watching too much TV. □ *I'm afraid Jimmy's becoming square-eyed from watching too much television.* □ *Another classroom of square-eyed little monsters again, the teacher thought.*

squashy bits a feminine euphemism for the breasts. (Crude.) □ *Hey! Mind my squashy bits with that door!* □ *There I stood, my hands trying to hide my squashy bits, screaming at him to get out of the room.*

squidgy 1. soggy or damp. □ *Jimmy! How did you get all your clothes all squidgy like this?* □ *It was another horrible, squidgy day.*

2. squeezable. □ *This new material is very squidgy, as you will see.* □ *Squidgy things are more "friendly" than hard ones.*

squire a jocular term of address between men. □ *Morning, squire!* □ *How can I help you today, squire?*

squit 1. a small or unimportant person. □ *He's a pleasant little squit.* □ *The squit was waiting outside the office for him.* **2.** to exterminate; to destroy. □ *Why should anyone want to squit this great venture?* □ *I think he's trying to squit us.*

squiz a brief glance. □ *He took a squiz but saw nothing unusual.* □ *Take a squiz at that!*

staunch someone very keen on sports and other outdoors activities, and who makes life unpleasant for those who are not so inclined. □ *Why do I seem to be surrounded by staunches in this place?* □ *A staunch? Me? You're joking!*

steam 1. to rush through a public place or vehicle such as a train, robbing all there. □ *A gang steamed the tube train and got away with a few hundred quid.* □ *Have you ever steamed anywhere?* **2.** to work very hard. □ *We must really steam this one right now. There is no time to lose!* □ *If you steam like crazy you should be finished on time.* **3.** to travel rapidly, by any means of transportation. □ *If you must steam like that you'll get booked.* □ *Steaming around on a motorbike can be dangerous.* **4.** old-fashioned; traditional; trustworthy. □ *Why do we have to deal with steam people all the time?* □ *I don't know why, but I prefer the steam railway to the modern electric one.*

steamer 1. one who robs by steaming. □ *I think he's one of the steamers who did the tube train, sir.* □ *When did you become a steamer then, son?* **2.** a cigarette. (Teens.) □ *He produced a steamer and lit it.* □ *I threw my steamer away and turned to look him in the eye.*

steam radio a jocular name for radio since the arrival of television. □ *Yes he's broadcast, but only on steam radio.* □ *An amazing number remain loyal to steam radio, you know.*

steam tug a foolish person. (Rhyming slang, linked as follows: steam tug ≈ [mug] = fool.) □ *How can you be such a steam tug?* □ *Making a steam tug like that of someone is not funny.*

steever five pence; originally, a one shilling coin. □ *That'll be a steever, missus.* □ *A steever? For what? That's a lot!*

stick 1. the device used to propel the ball in various games, such as golf, hockey, billiards, etc. □ *These aren't my sticks, and you aren't my caddy. What's going on around this golf club today?* □ *Joan, our little hockey player, wanted a new stick for her birthday, but got a coat instead.* **2.** a joystick. (The principal attitude control column of an aircraft.) □ *The pilot pulled back on the stick, and the plane did nothing—being that he hadn't even started the engine or anything yet.* □ *You pull back on the stick, which lowers the tail and raises the nose, and up you go.* **3.** punishment; censure; criticism. □ *That tyke! I'll give him some stick he won't forget in a hurry!* □ *Is it really necessary to dole out as much stick as you do?* **4.** a small glass of beer. □ *Give my friend here a stick.* □ *How about a stick before you go, Charlie?*

stick at trifles to let small details get in the way of a larger issue; to become bogged down with trivia. □ *There are important matters here and we don't want to stick at trifles.* □ *Many a major deal has come unstuck by sticking at trifles.*

stick it on someone to punch someone. □ *Tom stuck it on Fred on the hooter.* □ *She tried to stick it on me!*

sticky end an unpleasant or messy way to die. □ *Julius Caesar came to a sticky end on the steps of the Capitol.* □ *If you don't get that report on my desk by morning, you'll be coming to a sticky end, too!*

sticky wicket 1. a cricket pitch that has not yet dried after rain and so is difficult to play. □ *I think we'll have a sticky wicket after that rain.* □ *The sticky wicket made the game slow for the rest of the day.* **2.** a difficult situation. □ *How did we get into a sticky wicket like this?* □ *We've got a bit of a sticky wicket here.*

sting 1. a confidence trick. □ *That street trader caught me in a very neat sting. Unfortunately.* □ *Take care, most pawnshops work some kind of sting on their punters.* **2.** a scheme intended to entrap criminals. □ *The sting came off without a hitch.* □ *It was a well-planned sting and shouldn't have failed.* **3.** any short burst of music, a logo, or other sign used as a station identifier by a TV or radio station. □ *Here comes the sting for your soap, mum!* □ *I like the programme but hate the sting. Sorry.*

stitch up someone or something to deal with someone or something in an effective, thorough, final, but ruthless way. □ *They've really stitched me up now, that's for sure.* □ *We found a way to stitch up that little difficulty once and for all.*

St Louis blues 1. shoes. (Rhyming slang.) □ *Why are you in your St Louis blues? Are you going somewhere?* □ *I find these St Louis blues uncomfortable.* **2.** news. (Rhyming slang. Scots usage.) □ *What's the St Louis blues, Wullie?* □ *You could tell he was the bearer of bad St Louis blues.*

stockbroker belt the prosperous suburbs where stockbrokers live. □ *He's got a huge house in the stockbroker belt, you know.* □ *We're moving to the stockbroker belt ourselves, you know.*

Stockbroker Tudor expensive, but tasteless, reproduction architecture. □ *As you might expect, Gloria lives in a typical example of Stockbroker Tudor.* □ *Stockbroker Tudor may not be to your taste, but it is not cheap.*

stodge thick, heavy, unappetising food. □ *This stuff is just stodge.* □ *Have you nothing but stodge in this place?*

Stone me! AND **Stone the crows!** an exclamation of surprise. □ *Stone me! He didn't, did he?* □ *Well stone the crows, what do you expect!*

Stone the crows! See Stone me!

stonewall bonkers absolutely certain. □ *It's stonewall bonkers. Everything is now settled.* □ *Can you have two? For stonewall bonkers you can!*

stop a packet to be killed or wounded, especially by a bullet. □ *My great-uncle stopped a packet during the Battle of the Somme.* □ *If you go out into that firefight, you're almost sure to stop a packet.*

stop at home to stay at home. □ *No, I'm not going. I'm stopping at home tonight.* □ *Can we not both stop at home tomorrow, dear?*

stormer a large or impressive entity. □ *Boy, there's a real stormer!* □ *We're looking for a stormer here.*

straight from the bog AND **straight off the turnips** as Irish as can be. (Offensive.) □ *Here they are, more Irish straight from the bog!* □ *They don't all come straight off the turnips, you know. They are intelligent and well educated.*

straight off the turnips See straight from the bog.

strangler a necktie. □ *Pardon me sir, is this your strangler?* □ *The attacker was wearing a bright strangler, constable.*

strawberry 1. a red nose. □ *How did you get a strawberry like that?* □ *He threatened to punch me right on my big strawberry!* **2.** a cripple. (Rhyming slang, linked as follows: strawberry [ripple] ≈ cripple. Strawberry ripple is a variety of ice cream.) □ *You can't go around calling people with walking difficulties strawberries!* □ *I would not say he's a strawberry, but he has great difficulty with walking.*

streets ahead much superior. □ *What Jones Co. has to offer is streets ahead of anything from Smith Ltd.* □ *Don't worry, you're streets ahead of the competition.*

Strike a light! an exclamation of surprise. □ *Well strike a light, what do you expect!* □ *Strike a light! He didn't, did he?*

strike(-me) bread. (Rhyming slang, linked as follows: strike(-me) [dead] ≈ bread.) □ *Any strike-me, love?* □ *Even a few slices of strike would be good.*

stroppy obstreperous. □ *Oh, he's always being stroppy about something or other.* □ *I don't want that stroppy character working here.*

struggle and strife a wife. (Rhyming slang.) □ *My struggle and strife disapproved of the film.* □ *I've got to go home to me struggle and strife.*

stubs the teeth. □ *Look at her nice white stubs!* □ *I've got to go and brush my stubs.*

stumper a wicket keeper. (Cricket.) □ *Who's to be stumper?* □ *The stumper caught him!*

stump up to pay up. □ *I refuse to stump up for someone else's stupidity.* □ *You know, you're going to have to stump up anyway in the long run.*

subcheese everything; the lot. (From the Hindi words *sab* and *chiz*, meaning "all" and "thing" respectively, by hobson-jobson.) □ *Yes. Everything, the lot, subcheese.* □ *You can have the subcheese so far as I care.*

subtopia ugly and unplanned urban or suburban sprawl. □ *Everywhere there was subtopia, to the horizon.* □ *He hated living in subtopia but everyone did. What could he do?*

sunny south the mouth. (Rhyming slang.) □ *How do we get her sunny south closed so the rest can talk?* □ *Why don't you just close your sunny south for a moment and listen.*

sunshine a jocular term of address for a man or boy. (The term has no racial implications and is derived from *son*.) □ *You think you're so smart, don't you, sunshine?* □ *Look, sunshine, just watch yourself, all right?*

supergrass a police informer supplying information or evidence that is especially incriminating or concerns a large number of people. □ *They say that after giving evidence, the supergrass had plastic surgery, was provided with a new identity, and relocated to Australia.* □ *One supergrass and we could get the lot, sir.*

suss 1. a suspect. (Police.) □ *Right, let's interview our suss.* □ *Bring the suss in now, constable.* **2.** suspicion. (Police.) □ *We told the inspector of our suss about the bloke's story.* □ *If you've got good grounds for your suss, we'll take this further.* **3.** [appearing] suspicious. (Police.) □ *It looks kinda suss to me, sarge.* □ *If you think it's really suss, pull them in.* **4.** to suspect something. □ *Keep everything normal. I don't want her to suss anything. She has never had a surprise party before.* □ *He sussed something the minute he came into the room.*

sussy suspicious. □ *Something about the deal seemed sussy.* □ *Barlowe squinted a bit. Something was sussy here, he thought.*

swag someone away to kidnap or abduct someone. (Police.) □ *Looks like they've managed to swag her away after all.* □ *No one's going to get off with swagging anyone away while I'm in charge around here.*

swallow and sigh a collar and tie. (Rhyming slang.) □ *You've got to have on a swallow and sigh to get in there.* □ *He hates wearing a swallow and sigh.*

swan around to move around in a casual way while presenting a superior attitude to others. □ *I could not swan around like that all day long.* □ *There he was, swanning around as usual.*

swankpot someone who behaves in an ostentatious manner. □ *Why do we need this swankpot?* □ *Ask the swankpot if he needs any help.*

swear and cuss a bus. (Rhyming slang.) □ *Waiting for the swear and cuss, eh?* □ *I met him on the swear and cuss this morning.*

swear blind to affirm in a very forceful and convincing manner. □ *I swear blind I had nothing to do with it!* □ *You can swear blind if you like. Your fingerprints say different.*

the **Sweeney (Todd)** a police flying squad, especially in London. (Rhyming slang, derived from Sweeney Todd, an early-19th-century London barber convicted of murdering his clients.) □ *The Sweeney Todd is London's top crime-busting unit.* □ *Send for the Sweeney!*

sweet and sours flowers. (Rhyming slang.) □ *What does it say when it's the girl who brings the boy sweet and sours?* □ *A huge bunch of sweet and sours were waiting for her when she got home.*

sweet evening cheese. (Rhyming slang, linked as follows: sweet evening [breeze] ≈ cheese.) □ *Can I have some sweet evening, please?* □ *He likes a few biscuits with his sweet evening.*

sweetie a small item of sweet confectionery. □ *Mummy, can I have a sweetie?* □ *I love sweeties. I always have, ever since I was little.*

swift unfair. □ *Hey, that's swift!* □ *I'm not letting you be swift like that.*

swiftie AND **swift one** a quick drink. □ *You know how a swiftie disagrees with you, my dear.* □ *I often enjoy a swift one in the evening.*

swift one See swiftie.

swish 1. elegant; fashionable; attractive and smart. □ *Oh, you do look swish today!* □ *What a swish dress that is.* **2.** effeminate. (Crude.) □ *Why does he have to behave in such a swish way?* □ *A swish man does not have to be gay, you know!*

swizz(le) 1. something that is unfair. □ *My last job was a swizz. I hope this is better.* □ *You really got a swizzle there.* **2.** a swindle. □ *They pulled a real dirty swizz on that old lady.* □ *This is an okay swizzle you've got going here.*

swot a hard-working, serious pupil or student. □ *Yes, he's a swot, and he passes his exams, too.* □ *I wouldn't like to be a swot.*

syrup a wig. (Rhyming slang, linked as follows: syrup [of figs] ≈ wig.) □ *I wear just a little syrup to cover up a shiny spot.* □ *Is that guy wearing a syrup, or does his scalp really slide from side to side?*

ta an infantile form of *thank you*, also used informally by adults. □ *Ta for the coffee.* □ *Yes, the meal you bought. Ta.*

tab See yomp.

tacker a child. □ *She is a most irritating tacker, I'm afraid.* □ *Is this tacker yours?*

tag on to something AND **twig (on to) something; take something on board** to comprehend something. □ *Don't worry, he'll tag on to this eventually.* □ *I think I've taken this on board now.*

take a nosy around to take a look around. □ *I think I'll take a nosy around.* □ *The detective inspector is just taking a nosy around, sir.*

take a pew See grab a pew.

take a purler to be hit in such a way as to fall lengthways. □ *I took a purler and was in hospital for a week.* □ *Clear off, or I'll make sure you take a purler you won't forget in a hurry!*

take a shufti to take a look. □ *Cor! Take a shufti at this!* □ *We each took a shufti, but really there was little to see.*

take someone or something off to mimic or parody someone or something. (Usually in a mocking fashion.) □ *The comedian took off the wealthy politician.* □ *Well, I took off the dean, but it didn't go down too well.*

take something on board 1. to accept or seriously consider an idea. □ *I don't think she had ever seriously taken that idea on board until now.* □ *Try to take this point on board. It may save your business.* **2.** to accept responsibility for something. □ *Please take it on board. After all, you did it.* □ *All right, I've taken it on board. It's my fault.* **3.** See tag on to something.

take the biscuit AND **take the bun; take the cake** to be exceptional or remarkable. □ *I think that idea really must take the biscuit.* □ *It takes the cake for him to say a thing like that.*

take the bun See take the biscuit.

take the cake See take the biscuit.

talk nineteen to the dozen to talk in a rapid and continuous stream. □ *They were all talking nineteen to the dozen when we arrived.* □ *If we all talk nineteen to the dozen nothing will get done.*

talk one's head off to talk endlessly; to argue at length or vigorously. □ *I talked my head off trying to convince them.* □ *Don't waste time talking your head off to them.*

talk wet to speak in a foolishly sentimental way. □ *Don't talk wet!* □ *Talking wet like that is stupid.*

tank 1. a drink of beer, usually a pint. □ *Can I have a tank please?* □ *I do like this tank they have in here.* **2.** to travel at a high speed. □ *We were tanking along the motorway when this cop car spotted us.* □ *She tanked past me a few miles back. What's up?*

tat 1. a grubby individual. □ *The guy is a real tat, I'm afraid.* □ *You stupid tat!* **2.** garbage or junk. □ *She looked around the room and said she could never live with all that tat.* □ *This stuff is just tat. Show me something better.* **3.** clothes lacking taste. □ *He's the one dressed in tat.* □ *Why are you always dressed in such terrible tat?*

taters cold weather. (Rhyming slang, linked as follows: taters = [potatoes in the mould] ≈ cold weather.) □ *When it's taters like this, I try to avoid going outdoors.* □ *I know it's taters, but someone has to do it.*

tea grout a boy scout. (Rhyming slang.) □ *What is that tea grout doing?* □ *Were you ever a tea grout?*

tea leaf a thief. (Rhyming slang.) □ *We are the police. We are here to catch tea leaves, madam.* □ *This little beggar is just another tea leaf.*

tear a strip off someone to reprimand someone. □ *Misbehave and he'll tear a strip off you for sure.* □ *The teacher tore a strip off the wayward pupil.*

tearaway 1. a juvenile delinquent. □ *Jerry is a real tearaway. Look what he did!* □ *Who's the tearaway who has ruined all my work?*

2. an unthinking or careless youth. □ *Who's that tearaway I saw Linda with?* □ *I don't like him, he's nothing but a tearaway!*

Tea's up. Here is tea ready to drink. □ *Tea's up! Come and get it!* □ *Come on, tea's up.*

telephone numbers vast sums of money. □ *She gets paid telephone numbers to worry about stuff like that.* □ *To me, £400 is almost telephone numbers!*

telly 1. a television set. □ *Have you seen the rubbish they put on the telly these days?* □ *What's showing on the telly tonight?* **2.** television. (The medium.) □ *The influence of telly is almost impossible to exaggerate.* □ *I like the telly.*

ten a penny AND **two a penny** very common. □ *Skirts like that are ten a penny.* □ *Her type are as common as they come—two a penny.*

ten bob bit a fifty pence coin. (From this value in pre-1971 currency.) □ *He chucked her a ten bob bit and left.* □ *I hate these ten bob bits, they're so big and bulky.*

tenner a ten pound note. (Compare with **fiver.**) □ *For a tenner, the tramp led Barlowe to the place where the crate still lay in the alley.* □ *Barlowe slipped him a tenner and faded into the fog.*

ten penn'orth a prison sentence of ten years. □ *Oh no, ten penn'orth. I could not believe I could be so unlucky.* □ *The judge said he was sorry he wasn't able to send him away for more than a ten penn'orth.*

test a cricket test match. □ *Harry likes to watch tests on the TV.* □ *When is the next test?*

That's (gone and) torn it! See **That tears it!**

That's what I say (too). I agree with you. □ *Of course, Mary. That's what I say.* □ *That's what I say, too. The way to cut spending is just to do it.*

That tears it! AND **That's (gone and) torn it!** That has ruined everything!; Everything is wrecked now! □ *Well, that tears it! I'm leaving!* □ *I thought yesterday's error was bad enough, but that's gone and torn it now!*

there you are a public house or pub. (Rhyming slang, linked as follows: there you are ≈ [bar] = pub(lic house).) □ *He's down* *the there you are, as usual.* □ *That's not a bad little there you are you've got there, mate.*

thimble and thumb rum. (Rhyming slang.) □ *I could use a thimble and thumb.* □ *The thimble and thumb were certainly flowing that evening, I can tell you.*

third wicket partnership a pair of cricketing batsmen working together to make runs. □ *The two of them made a magnificent third wicket partnership.* □ *That was a terrible performance. These two are no more a third wicket partnership than my aunt and the cat next door.*

this and that See ball and bat.

three'd up having three prisoners in one cell. (Prison.) □ *Yes, we were three'd up for a few months. It was pretty grim.* □ *Prison is bad always, but three'd up it becomes much worse still.*

throw a wobbly to suddenly or unexpectedly behave irrationally. □ *Well the opposition have really thrown a wobbly this time.* □ *I wonder what caused him to throw a wobbly like that?*

thundering vast or considerable. □ *Why are lawyers' fees always so thundering big?* □ *A thundering great aircraft flew low over the village.*

thunder-thighs someone who is grossly overweight. (Crude.) □ *Here comes old thunder-thighs.* □ *Here, thunder-thighs, let me get you a chair or two.*

tick 1. a minute; a second; a brief interval of time. (Originally, the time between two ticks of a clock.) □ *I'll be with you in a tick.* □ *This won't take a tick. Sit tight.* **2.** credit. □ *I suppose we could buy it on tick.* □ *It costs more on tick, you know.*

tickety-boo AND **ticketty-boo; tiggerty-boo** all right; okay; correct; satisfactory. (Possibly from the Hindustani *tikai babu,* meaning "it is all right, sir," in which case the expression is an example of hobson-jobson.) □ *It's fine. It's all tickety-boo.* □ *Don't worry, it's all tiggerty-boo again now.*

tick over [for a person, business, machine, etc.] to operate at a minimal level. □ *After his illness he's really just ticking over.* □ *Let the car tick over until we're ready to go.*

tiger 1. a strong, aggressive, awe-inspiring person. (Usually male.) □ *The guy's a tiger. Take care.* □ *Isn't Brian a tiger when he's* *roused!* **2.** a wife. □ *The tiger is angry with me.* □ *I've got to get home to the tiger.*

tiggerty-boo See tickety-boo.

timbers cricket stumps or wickets. □ *The ball went clean through the timbers.* □ *At close of play we pull the timbers and bring them back to the clubhouse.*

tin money. □ *How much tin do you need, then?* □ *Sorry, I can't afford it, I've no tin.*

tin lid 1. the **tin lid** the last straw. □ *When she poured her drink down my back, that was the tin lid.* □ *This is just the tin lid. I'm leaving.* **2.** a child. (Rhyming slang, linked as follows: tin lid ≈ [kid] = child.) □ *Our tin lid is playing in the garden.* □ *How many tin lids do you have now?*

tin plate a friend. (Rhyming slang, linked as follows: tin plate ≈ [mate] = friend.) □ *The two tin plates left the pub, each one preventing the other from falling over.* □ *Who's your tin plate, Albert?*

tin tack 1. a sack. (Rhyming slang.) □ *He opened the tin tack and looked inside.* □ *What's in yer tin tack, mate?* **2.** a job dismissal; the sack. (Rhyming slang.) □ *The boss gave them all the tin tack.* □ *The tin tack is what I am afraid of.*

tin termites rust (on a car). □ *I see the thing's infested with tin termites.* □ *Everywhere you looked, the tin termites had eaten away at the bodywork.*

tiswas a state of chaos or confusion. □ *No more tiswas like that, thank you very much.* □ *What a tiswas there is in that office. I don't know how they can ever get anything done.*

titfer a hat. (Rhyming slang, linked as follows: titfer ≈ [tit-for-tat] ≈ hat.) □ *I'm going to buy myself a new titfer.* □ *Why are you wearing that ridiculous titfer?*

tit willow AND **weeping willow** a pillow. (Rhyming slang.) □ *As soon as her head hit the tit willow she was sound asleep.* □ *Can I have another weeping willow, please?*

toby 1. a tramp. □ *Two old tobies wandered slowly down the lane.* □ *The toby asked politely for some work that he would be paid for in food.* **2.** a young child. (Also a term of address.) □ *Is this toby yours?* □ *She is a most irritating toby.*

toffee nonsense. □ *That's just a lot of toffee. Ignore it.* □ *Boy, he can certainly churn out toffee by the ton!*

tog up to dress up. □ *Oh good, I like togging up.* □ *We all got togged up before the party.*

tom-cat doormat. (Rhyming slang.) □ *Clean your feet on the tom-cat.* □ *Someone had removed the tom-cat.*

tom(foolery) jewellery. (Rhyming slang.) □ *She's out tonight with all the tomfoolery on.* □ *Don't wear your tom out in the street, love. You'll lose it.*

Tom(, Harry,) and Dick sick. (Rhyming slang.) □ *If you're Tom, Harry, and Dick, we better stop.* □ *I told you that curry would make you Tom and Dick.*

Tommy Rabbit a pomegranate. (Rhyming slang.) □ *The coster-monger's stall was laden with every sort of fruit, even the occasional Tommy Rabbit.* □ *Have you ever tasted a Tommy Rabbit?*

Tom Thumb the buttocks. (Rhyming slang, linked as follows: Tom Thumb ≈ [bum] = buttocks.) □ *He got arrested trying to look up women's skirts in the hope of seeing their Tom Thumbs.* □ *If your dresses get any shorter, we'll all be able to see your Tom Thumb.*

ton 1. a score of 100 in a game such as darts. □ *I bet he can't make a ton in one turn.* □ *Two double twenties and a single one. Just like that, he scored a ton!* **2.** one hundred pounds sterling. □ *Can you lend me a ton till pay-day?* □ *All right, here's a ton. Don't spend it all in one shop.*

toot money. (Rhyming slang, linked as follows: toot ≈ [loot] = money.) □ *It takes a lot of toot to buy a car like that.* □ *I don't make enough toot to go on a trip like that!*

top and tail 1. to cook and preserve fruit, etc. □ *It's important to top and tail fruit when it's ready. It won't wait.* □ *My wife is in the kitchen, topping and tailing the fruit from our garden.* **2.** to wash and check over a bedridden patient. (Hospital.) □ *Nurse Smith, top and tail that patient, please.* □ *I'm exhausted! I've been topping and tailing patients all day!*

top-hole excellent. □ *Boy, this fishing rod is top-hole!* □ *This wine is really top-hole!*

top of the shop 1. the highest number called in a game of bingo, lotto, tombola, or another lottery-like game. □ *Harry got the top* *of the shop in that game.* □ *There's a prize for the top of the shop this time.* **2.** the very best quality item on sale in a shop. □ *Only the top of the shop for you, my dear!* □ *Shopkeeper, bring out the top of the shop for us to see!*

top storey AND **upper storey (department)** the brain. □ *A little lightweight in the upper storey department, but other than that, a great guy.* □ *He has nothing for a top storey.*

tosh 1. money. □ *Sorry, I can't afford it, I've no tosh.* □ *How much tosh do you need, then?* **2.** nonsense. □ *What tosh that is!* □ *You're talking tosh again—as usual.*

tot 1. a shot of liquor. □ *Fancy a tot?* □ *He knocked back one tot and asked for another.* **2.** discarded items rescued by a rubbish collector for his own delectation. □ *And just what are you going to do with all this tot?* □ *You've certainly got a lot of tot in here.*

tote something up See notch something up.

touch someone or something with a bargepole to deal with or handle someone or something. (Always in the negative.) □ *I wouldn't touch that problem with a bargepole.* □ *Mr Wilson is a real pain, and I wouldn't touch his account with a bargepole. Find somebody else to handle it.*

touch wood to knock on wood, as a talisman of good luck. □ *We should be all right now, touch wood.* □ *Touch wood, and then let's get going again.*

trap 1. See claptrap. **2. traps** one's personal effects or trappings. □ *I've come to collect my traps.* □ *All my traps will fit into one small suitcase.*

trimmer a prevaricator; an equivocator. □ *He's always been a trimmer and won't change now.* □ *We don't want a trimmer but someone who can make decisions.*

trog a lout. □ *Tell that trog we don't want him here any more.* □ *Who's that trog kicking at the side of your car?*

trog along to trudge or plod, as when carrying a heavy load. □ *We had to help. She was trogging along in the rain with two heavy suitcases.* □ *I do feel sorry for anyone having to trog along like that.*

trolleys See trollies.

trollies AND **trolleys 1.** a woman's panties or knickers. (Crude. Always in the plural.) □ *She went to the shops and bought herself* *some new trollies.* □ *Oh heavens she thought, as she stepped off the bus. I've forgotten my trollies!* **2.** a man's underpants. (Always in the plural.) □ *Truly! He was wearing luminous, glow-in-the-dark trollies!* □ *There's a whole drawer there just full of my trollies.*

trombone a telephone. (Rhyming slang.) □ *He's got one of them portable trombones.* □ *You'll find a trombone over in that corner.*

tronk an idiot. □ *Don't be a tronk. That's impossible.* □ *Who's the tronk in the bright orange trousers?*

tross to walk. (Post Office.) □ *The postman trosses his round here.* □ *This delivery route is too long to tross.*

trot nonsense. □ *Don't give me that trot! I won't buy it.* □ *That's just a lot of trot.*

trouble and strife AND **worry and strife** one's wife. (Rhyming slang. Compare with **old bubble.**) □ *Will your trouble and strife let you out to the pub tonight?* □ *I'd better ask the worry and strife.*

tube 1. AND the **Tube** London's underground railway system. □ *Millions of Londoners depend on the Tube to get to work every morning.* □ *The Tube is one of the most extensive underground railway systems in the world.* **2.** the **tube** a television set. □ *What's on the tube tonight?* □ *The tube is on the blink, so I read a book.* **3.** a submarine. □ *That's my tube, against that jetty over there.* □ *There is something rather sinister about the black hull of a nuclear tube gliding silently through the water.*

tuck food, especially confectionery and cakes eaten by children. (An abbreviation of the obsolete British—but contemporary Australian—slang word *tucker,* meaning "food.") □ *What tuck have you got today?* □ *I'm not sharing my tuck with anyone.*

tuck in to eat up eagerly. □ *After Christmas, we tucked in to turkey for three days.* □ *Who's been tucking in on the chocolate cake?*

tumble down the sink a drink. (Rhyming slang.) □ *I was in the pub having a quiet tumble down the sink when he came in.* □ *Let a man finish his tumble down the sink in peace first, okay?*

tuppenny-halfpenny practically worthless, almost without value. □ *Why are you bothering with such tuppenny-halfpenny stuff?* □ *Oh, he's just another tuppenny-halfpenny guy. Forget him.*

turn on a sixpence to turn sharply; to turn in a small radius. □ *This vehicle will turn on a sixpence.* □ *A car that will turn on a sixpence at high speed without turning turtle is what I want.*

turn queer to become somewhat unwell. □ *Something she ate turned her queer.* □ *Thinking of that could make me turn queer.*

turn up trumps 1. to be very helpful. □ *Thank you. You've turned up trumps!* □ *Thank you for turning up trumps yet again.* **2.** to unexpectedly resolve difficulties. □ *Well, I did not think he would turn up trumps like that.* □ *We certainly turned up trumps that time!* **3.** to perform better than expected. □ *As I might have expected, Walter has turned up trumps again.* □ *You had better turn up trumps this time, or face serious trouble.*

turtle-dove a glove. (Rhyming slang.) □ *Here she comes, wearing her turtle-doves as usual.* □ *If you're going to do that sort of heavy and dirty work, turtle-doves would be an excellent idea.*

twallop AND **twollop** a fool. □ *Those twallops are at it again. Spend, spend, spend.* □ *How can you be such a twollop?*

twee 1. affected; over-dainty; quaint. (Usually referring to a woman.) □ *She's a real twee type. You know—untouched by real life in any way.* □ *Fiona's far too twee ever to make a difficult choice.* **2.** excessively fastidious about neatness; disdainful of normal standards. □ *You will find that Lavinia is really very twee.* □ *I can't stand twee people.*

twig a style or custom. □ *I don't think that twig suits her.* □ *That is a strange twig they have around here.*

twig (on to) something See tag on to something.

twink a moment. □ *It only took a twink, but it was enough.* □ *A twink later it was all over.*

twinkle(s) jewellery. □ *Don't wear your twinkles out in the street, love. You'll lose the stuff.* □ *She's out tonight with all the twinkle on.*

twister 1. a key. (Underworld.) □ *Did you get the twister for this place, Max?* □ *Bruno lifted the jailer's twisters and hid them until midnight before trying anything.* **2.** a cheat or swindle. □ *Another twister like that and I call your parents.* □ *That little twister the kids did with the statue from the town square was a dandy.* **3.** a cricket ball bowled with a spin. □ *You're going to get twisters from this bowler.* □ *The bowler sent him a vicious twister.*

two a penny See ten a penny.

two eyes of blue absolutely correct. (Rhyming slang, linked as follows: two eyes of blue ≈ [(too) true] = absolutely correct.) □ *That's two eyes of blue, mate.* □ *You really expect us to believe that's two eyes of blue?*

twofer a cigarette. (From the slot machines that once—long ago—issued two cigarettes for one penny.) □ *Hey, give me a twofer, eh?* □ *I'll trade you a twofer for a light.*

twollop See twallop.

twopenny the head. (Rhyming slang, linked as follows: twopenny [loaf] = [loaf of bread] ≈ head. It's a long time since a loaf cost two pennies; this expression is showing its age.) □ *Where'd you get that nasty bump on your twopenny?* □ *Harry's distinctive hairy twopenny hove into view.*

twopenny damn that which is worthless. (Crude.) □ *I don't give a twopenny damn what you think.* □ *It's just not worth a twopenny damn. OK?*

two-up, two-down a house with two rooms on each of its two floors. □ *We bought a little two-up, two-down because it was all we could afford at the time.* □ *It may be no more than a two-up, two-down, but it's a very nice two-up, two-down.*

typewriter a fighter; a boxer. (Rhyming slang, linked as follows: typewriter ≈ [fighter] = boxer.) □ *I tell you, Mr Big, this one is a real typewriter.* □ *With a typewriter like him we can make serious money.*

U

ugsome unpleasant without any redeeming features. □ *Now that was one ugsome film.* □ *He stood before the ugsome building and shuddered.*

Uncle (Dick) sick. (Rhyming slang.) □ *God, I feel really Uncle Dick!* □ *Paul was feeling Uncle so I sent him home.*

Uncle Fred bread. (Rhyming slang.) □ *What, there's nothing to eat? Not even Uncle Fred?* □ *She got out the Uncle Fred and cut off a few slices.*

Uncle Ned 1. a bed. (Rhyming slang.) □ *Somebody put a spider in my Uncle Ned.* □ *I was so tired I could hardly find my Uncle Ned.* **2.** a head. (Rhyming slang.) □ *He's distinctive because he has a particularly large Uncle Ned.* □ *Turn your Uncle Ned around and take a look at this.*

Uncle Willy 1. silly. (Rhyming slang.) □ *Y'know, maybe that's not so Uncle Willy.* □ *Come on, don't be Uncle Willy.* **2.** chilly. (Rhyming slang.) □ *Sonia hates it when it's Uncle Willy like this.* □ *In Uncle Willy weather he prefers to stay indoors.*

underfug underclothes. (Childish.) □ *Johnny, put your underfug back on.* □ *I don't like my underfug.*

underkecks underpants. □ *First, let's get you out of these tattered underkecks.* □ *How could anyone wear dirty, worn-out underkecks like that?*

unhappy chappie someone, usually male, who is extremely displeased. □ *There's an extremely unhappy chappie in the front office asking for you, Cynthia.* □ *Being Complaints Officer does mean that it's you that deals with unhappy chappies, you know.*

uni university. □ *What are you reading at uni?* □ *He's a prof at the uni.*

unwaged 1. unemployed. □ *If you're unwaged, go over there.* □ *I'm unwaged, I'm afraid.* **2.** unpaid. □ *I don't do unwaged work.* □ *Why are we unwaged for this?*

up one's street See right up one's street.

upper storey (department) See top storey.

upsides with someone or something equivalent or equal to someone or something. □ *So you think that's the way to be upsides with Roger?* □ *You'll never get upsides with him because you're not half the man.*

up the spout 1. hopeless. □ *The cause is gone, lost, up the spout.* □ *Let's not say it's up the spout just yet. Ken's making one more try.* **2.** useless. □ *I am afraid the plan is completely up the spout. We must think again.* □ *Well, that's it. The car's up the spout.* **3.** pawned. □ *You'd be amazed at some of the things you'd find up the spout.* □ *Everything I have is already up the spout.* **4.** destroyed. □ *It's all useless, all up the spout!* □ *It's all up the spout again.*

vox pop comments made by individual members of the public, purporting to represent public opinion on a radio or TV show. (From the Latin *vox populi*, meaning "voice of the people.") □ *We got a lot of vox pop on this show, and it was all negative.* □ *Who cares what the vox pop says? I loved it!*

W

waffle nonsensical talk. □ *Don't talk waffle.* □ *If you just come out with waffle, you'll be ignored.*

Wait a mo! Wait a moment! □ *Wait a mo! You can't leave it like that!* □ *Wait a mo! Something is happening!*

Wake up your ideas! Get your thinking sorted out!; Think more clearly! □ *If you want this to work, wake up your ideas!* □ *Wake up your ideas or let someone else have a go!*

walk it to win with ease. (Originally of a horse race.) □ *Come on! You'll walk it!* □ *I knew you would walk it.*

wamba money. □ *I don't make enough wamba to go on a trip like that!* □ *It takes a lot of wamba to buy a car like that.*

wang disgusting food. □ *That stuff is just wang.* □ *Call that wang food?*

wangle an illicit favour. □ *Can you work a wangle for me, mate?* □ *I don't like all these wangles. One day we'll be caught.*

wasp a traffic warden. □ *I was only one minute over, but still the wasp issued the ticket.* □ *Wasps must get insulted by drivers all day long.*

Watcher! Look out! □ *Watcher, mate! You all right?* □ *Watcher! Mind that ladder!*

water-hen ten. (Rhyming slang.) □ *A water-hen? You've got that many?* □ *I'll give you a quid for water-hen of them.*

wazzock 1. a stupid or incapable person. (Offensive. Also a term of address.) □ *What a wazzock that woman can be.* □ *Get out of here, you wazzock!* **2.** a drunkard. □ *You are going to turn into a real wazzock if you don't let up on your drinking.* □ *There was some wazzock asleep across the front entrance to the office when I got here this morning.*

wedge a sandwich. □ *Can I have a wedge, mum?* □ *He sat there, eating a wedge.*

weeping willow See tit willow.

wellie AND **welly** a wellington boot. (Normally in the plural.) □ *Well, pull on your wellies and let's go for a walk across the field.* □ *Jimmy lost a welly when it got stuck in the mud.*

well-in popular. □ *She's a very well-in young lady around here, you know.* □ *If you're that well-in, you've nothing to worry about.*

well shod [of a car] with tyres in good condition. (This is hyphenated before a nominal.) □ *Now here's a well-shod motor, squire.* □ *At least the car was well shod. Everything else about it was rotten except the tyres.*

welly See wellie.

wheelie bin a large, wheeled rubbish can, sometimes issued by garbage-collection agencies to simplify their work. □ *You can usually see wheelie bins at the foot of these tower blocks.* □ *Someone tried to block the entranceway with a wheelie bin.*

wheeze a clever idea. □ *A few more wheezes like that and you've got it made!* □ *Here, that was a clever wheeze! How did you come up with that one!*

whennie a person who bores listeners with tales of past exploits. (From regular use of the expression "When I . . .") □ *Oh, he's a real whennie.* □ *That whennie has three basic stories, but they seem to bear endless repetition.*

when the balloon goes up when trouble starts. □ *When the balloon goes up I intend to be long gone.* □ *Are you ready for when the balloon goes up?*

whinge AND **winge** to complain repeatedly or continuously. □ *Some people whinge because they don't have anything else to do.* □ *Come on, don't winge all the time!*

whip-round an informal collection of money for a charitable cause of some sort. □ *Oh, you've got to put something into a whip-round for the hospice.* □ *Amazingly, the whip-round collected almost £1,000.*

whisper (and talk) a walk. (Rhyming slang.) □ *Go on! Get out! Take a whisper and talk!* □ *I went for a whisper, just to get away from him.*

whistle a suit of clothes. (Rhyming slang, linked as follows: whistle [and flute] ≈ suit (of clothes).) □ *I'll get on my whistle, and we'll go out tonight.* □ *You look pretty good in your new whistle.*

whochamaflip See who-d'ya-ma-flip.

who-d'ya-ma-flip AND **whochamaflip** someone whose name has been forgotten or was never known; someone whose name is being avoided. □ *Did you invite who-d'ya-ma-flip to the party?* □ *If you didn't invite whochamaflip, then who did?*

whole time full time. □ *She's in whole time work now.* □ *That's a whole time business nowadays, you know.*

whomp See whump.

whump AND **whomp** the sound made when two flat surfaces collide. □ *I heard the whump when the shed collapsed.* □ *The whomp woke everyone up.*

wide 1. shrewd or knowing, in a derogatory sense. □ *We don't need a wide individual in that job.* □ *Simon is a wide one all right. He knows all the tricks of the trade, which is just what worries me.* **2.** dishonest. □ *He's a wide one all right. Check your wallet before you leave.* □ *Get that wide boy out of here.* **3.** See wide boy.

wide (boy) a small-time crook. □ *Why do you hang around with these wide boys?* □ *He's just a wide, not worth worrying over.*

widget 1. a hypothetical product made by a hypothetical company. □ *Suppose two companies were to start manufacturing widgets.* □ *Can this company produce enough widgets to meet the demand?* **2.** any small gadget or device. □ *Do you have any more of these widgets?* □ *We need a special widget to make this work.*

wigging a scolding. □ *Her mother gave her a wigging when she finally got home.* □ *Tom got a wigging for his part in the prank.*

wind someone up 1. to irritate or provoke someone. □ *That remark really wound her up, once she realised what it meant.* □ *The whole business began to wind me up after a while.* **2.** to play a practical joke on someone. □ *Come on, you're winding me up.* □ *Would I wind you up? It's gospel!*

winge See whinge.

witch's hat a portable, plastic traffic cone. □ *There were thousands of witch's hats along the side of the road, ready for use.* □ *The car* *ran out of control into the work area, sending dozens of witch's hats flying in every direction.*

wolly a policeman in uniform. □ *Think about how the wolly on the beat is affected by this cold.* □ *The wolly stopped at the door, tried the lock, and moved on.*

womble anyone considered unfashionably dressed or uninteresting. (From a TV puppet show popular with young children in the 1970s.) □ *Oh, Sammy's just a womble.* □ *I don't want to be a womble. I want nice things to wear!*

wooden-eared See cloth-eared.

wooden ears See cloth ears.

wooden spoon See booby-prize.

woof one's custard to empty one's stomach; to vomit. (Crude.) □ *Fred is woofing his custard because of that lousy fish she served.* □ *One look at that food, and I wanted to woof my custard, too.*

woopsie an embarrassing error. □ *Woops! I've done another woopsie!* □ *That was a silly woopsie. I'm sorry.*

work a flanker (on someone) See do a flanker (on someone).

works outing a short pleasure-trip for employees, organised and usually paid for by their employer. □ *We're off on the works outing tomorrow.* □ *The annual works outing was a disaster. As usual.*

the **world and his wife** everybody. □ *It was as if the world and his wife were in our garden that afternoon.* □ *I thought this was a secret, but if you feel the world and his wife should know all about our private business, feel free.*

worry and strife See trouble and strife.

Wotcher! a friendly greeting between men. □ *Wotcher mate, how are you?* □ *Wotcher! OK, are you?*

wrinkly an old person. (Offensive. Also a term of address.) □ *Just remember we'll each of us be a wrinkly ourselves one day, with luck.* □ *Take care where there are wrinklies crossing the road.*

wrong 'un a dishonest person. □ *Let's face it, he's a wrong 'un.* □ *Even a wrong 'un has to earn a living, but honestly!*

X a written symbol of a kiss, sometimes found at the end of a letter sent between lovers. □ *I love you. XXXXXXX.* □ *Lots of love and Xs.*

yack (on) to chatter in an idle or meaningless fashion; to gossip. □ *He's always yacking on about something or other, but I like him.* □ *My, isn't Mary yacking a lot today?*

yank-tank a large American car. □ *Like my new yank-tank, darling?* □ *I'm rather partial to yank-tanks.*

the **Yard 1.** New Scotland Yard, the headquarters of the Metropolitan Police. □ *That's the Yard over there, son, where the coppers live.* □ *Do all the policemen really live in the Yard?* **2.** the Metropolitan Police. □ *The Yard are after me!* □ *The Yard finally caught up with the Streatham Strangler.*

Yarmouth capon See Billingsgate pheasant.

yatter to chatter at length about nothing much. □ *What are you yattering about now, woman?* □ *Yatter, yatter! That's all you ever do!*

yobbery hooliganism. □ *Something has to be done about all the yobbery we're getting around here nowadays.* □ *The police are determined to wipe out yobbery.*

yobbish in the manner of a hooligan. □ *Yobbish behaviour like that will get you in jail.* □ *We don't want yobbish youths like that in here.*

yob(bo) a lout or hooligan. (Backslang from *boy*.) □ *Who's that yobbo kicking at the side of your car?* □ *Tell that yob we don't want him here any more.*

yomp AND **tab** a forced military march in full kit. □ *It was the British Army yomp across the Falkland Islands that won that war.* □ *Right lads, there's a tab tomorrow.*

yonks a very long time; ages. □ *It's been like that for yonks.* □ *Just because it's not been changed for yonks is no reason not to change it now.*

you and me a cup of tea. (Rhyming slang.) □ *Ah, you and me! Always welcome.* □ *A cup of you and me was just what she needed.*

you lot all of you. □ *Right, you lot. Listen to what I have to say.* □ *You lot have got a lot of work to do.*

yummy See scrummy.

Z

zip(po) nothing. □ *There was nothing in the post today. Nothing. Zippo.* □ *I got zip from the booking agency all week.*

zizz a snooze or nap. □ *I need some zizz before I get started again.* □ *I could use a zizz before I have to get to work.*